27 VIEWS OF GREENSBORO

TANGER FAMILY BICENTENNIAL GARDEN

GUILFORD

Natthaniel Greene

CHILDREN'S MUSEUM

GREENSBORO LIBRARY

GREENSBORO COLLEGE

UNC-G

JEFFERSON PILOT BUILDING

NC A+T

BLANDWOOD

Depot

Bennett College

F.W. WOOLWORTH

CIVIL RIGHTS CENTER

27 Views of Greensboro

OF

GREENSBORO

The Gate City in Prose & Poetry

Introduction by Marianne Gingher

eno
publishers

27 Views of Greensboro: The Gate City in Prose & Poetry
Introduction by Marianne Gingher
© Eno Publishers, 2015
All rights reserved

 Eno Publishers
P.O. Box 158
Hillsborough, North Carolina 27278
www.enopublishers.org

ISBN-13: 978-0-9896092-1-0
ISBN-10: 0-98-960921-9
Library of Congress Control Number: 2015930674
First Edition, second printing

Cover illustration by Daniel Wallace, Chapel Hill, North Carolina
Design and typesetting by Horse & Buggy Press, Durham, North Carolina

Acknowledgments

www.ncarts.org

Eno Publishers wishes to acknowledge the generous support of the
North Carolina Arts Council's Program Support grant that helped
fund 27 *Views of Greensboro,* and other books in Eno's "27 Views" series.

The publisher also wishes to thank Gita Schonfeld, Speed Hallman, Caitlin
Whalen, Meg Williamson, and Adrienne Fox for their careful editorial work on the
views, and Daniel Wallace for his cover illustration.

A huge thank you to our Gate City authors and Introduction writer, Marianne
Gingher, who have created a literary montage of Greensboro, present and past.

Permissions

Some of the works in this volume have appeared in whole or in part in other publications.

"Another Culture," by Linda Beatrice Brown, is excerpted from *Belles of Liberty, Gender, Bennett College and the Civil Rights Movement in Greensboro, North Carolina*, Women and Wisdom Press, Greensboro NC, 2013.

Ed Cone's essay "Ghost City" builds on a column by the author published by the *News & Record* in 2005.

Table of Contents

❧ VIEWS FROM BEFORE

❧ A PLACE CALLED HOME

STREET SCENES

Preface

PERHAPS THE SUBTITLE of 27 *Views of Greensboro* should read *Mysteries of the Gate City Revealed.* If these streets could talk, if these neighborhoods, these houses, these walls could tell their stories . . . and they do in these pages. Twenty-seven authors delve into the complexities of life in the city named for a Revolutionary general who might have lost the Battle of Guilford Court House, but helped win the war.

27 *Views of Greensboro* is not a guide book in any traditional sense. It is a hometown anthology of writers writing about where they live. The views span genres (essays, creative nonfiction, poems, and a short story), as well as neighborhoods, decades, racial and cultural experiences, perspectives of born-and-raised Greensboroians and those who have adopted it as their home. Some views celebrate the city and its people, present and past; others expose its fissures, of race and history, of politics, of culture. Many views focus on change, the imperative of it, as well as its price.

Our hope is that this literary montage gives readers insight into life in the Gate City (and why it's called the Gate City) and how twenty-seven of its inhabitants think about the city they call home.

Elizabeth Woodman
Eno Publishers | Spring 2015

Introduction

GREENSBORO, NORTH CAROLINA—the Gate City, the 'Boro, Tournament Town—is home to nearly 270,000 souls—almost four times as many as when I moved here in 1950. More and more people find Greensboro attractive for any number of reasons. For a city its size, housing is still relatively cheap compared with other desirable North Carolina towns. My bungalow in Fisher Park would sell for twice its current market value if it were in Chapel Hill. Greensboro also offers all the benefits of a major metropolis without the traffic hassles. Driving anywhere in Greensboro— even in five o'clock traffic—is a breeze. Best of all is Greensboro's highly walkable downtown which still has a small-town vibe.

Downtown Greensboro has been making a "comeback" ever since modern shopping centers and malls began luring retail businesses to the suburbs sixty years ago or more. Strolling around recently, I'm keen to report that the city is molting buildings and reinventing itself even as I speak. Always has and always will, in the name of Progress. I discovered, for instance, that a huge swath on the northwestern edge of downtown proper has been flattened by bulldozers, taking down the historic Dixie Apartments, among other vintage properties, to make room for four acres of mixed-use development. I was on my way to Architectural Salvage on Bellemeade Street to shop for a retro pedestal sink only to arrive at a pile of rubble where Architectural Salvage had stood. Perplexed, I stopped in at Zito, a nearby wine shop, to find out what was happening and got an earful. There would be other casualties in the name of Progress, but the folks at Zito assured me that the wine shop would still be there next week. Farther southeast, three blocks from where I live and catty-cornered from the Greensboro Historical Museum, a performing arts center will soon be going up on a piece of land where the old Wesley Long Hospital once stood. When I was a kid, I got stitches there and had my stomach pumped.

Depending on the influence of civic leaders, decade to decade, Greensboro has suffered thoughtless bouts of tear-down-itis. Some downtown treasures have, thankfully, been preserved, like the gloriously refurbished Carolina Theatre, the handsome Jefferson Standard Building lording over the skyline (from my upstairs bedroom nearly a mile away, I can read the time and temperature flashing from its roof), and historic Woolworth's on Elm Street, where North Carolina A&T students held landmark sit-ins in 1960. I used to shop there as a kid looking for cheap thrills. But today, a guided tour of the building, now the International Civil Rights Center & Museum, is one of the most informative and potent Greensboro experiences to be had.

Greensboro boasts a spiffy downtown library, a central city park with fountains, and the Depot, Greensboro's train station, meticulously restored to early twentieth-century glamour. You half-expect a steam locomotive to arrive at the station platform with Humphrey Bogart and Ingrid Bergman on board. Fanning out from the city proper are five four-year colleges, the Tanger Family Bicentennial Garden, the Greensboro Science Center, and historic Guilford Courthouse National Military Park.

Factoids about Greensboro abound. It's called the Gate City, for instance, because of its importance as a railway hub and the expansion of its textile industry. Here are a few more: The official town of Greensboro was established by Quakers who, in the mid-1700s, settled at a nearby site called Capefair; for a brief period at the end of the Civil War, Greensboro became North Carolina's capital. Greensboro was spelled Greensborough until 1895; Greensboro actually has its own flag—green (no surprise there) with yellow lettering and a drawing of Nathanael Greene, the general

who defended us against British General Charles Cornwallis at the Battle
of Guilford Courthouse on March 15, 1781, and lost. Oops. If Greene lost,
why does the enemy Cornwallis have a street named for him? A nice street,
too, that runs through some of the poshest parts of town. The good news
for General Greene (he also has an important street named for him that
runs downtown, north to south) is that he inflicted such heavy losses
on Cornwallis that the British withdrew to lick their wounds at a base in
Wilmington.

Famous people born in Greensboro: the short story writer O. Henry
(well, actually he was born just outside Greensboro, in Guilford County,
but we are pleased to claim him); Dolley Madison, first lady and wife of
President James Madison; Doug Marlette, Pulitzer Prize-winning cartoon-
ist; Olympic speed skating Gold Medal-winner Joey Cheek; and a slew of
other professional sports figures. Edward R. Murrow, the famous pioneer
among television broadcast journalists, was born just outside Greensboro at Polecat Creek and lived in a log cabin there; Inez and Charlie Foxx,
a soul-singing duo known for their 1963 hit single "Mockingbird," hailed
from here, as did Donna Edmondson, Playmate of the Year, 1987.

If you seek a more thorough history of Greensboro, best to ask writer
Jim Schlosser who has written specifically, historically, and vividly about
every nuance of Greensboro his entire journalistic career, and writes in
these pages about Hamburger Square. Or ask the most erudite contem-
porary writer plunked down among us mortals here, Fred Chappell, also
a contributor to *27 Views of Greensboro*, who hasn't budged from the place
in decades. Or, for the most up-to-date wackiness that exists in this town,
read *O.Henry* magazine writer Maria Johnson, who's not relocating anywhere either. Her view here is about shopping for eternal real estate in the
city cemeteries.

I sometimes wonder why I have stayed in Greensboro when I might
have moved elsewhere. I want to better understand its pull on me, its webbing, its spiderland. Other longtime residents must feel it, too. I want to

detangle that webbing just a bit. After all, writers don't write simply to tell you things; they write to discover something they didn't know before. They write to know what they don't know about what they know, as Eudora Welty once put it, more or less.

My father had been raised in Greensboro, and my parents brought me back to settle in 1950. Our first house was a rental on Aberdeen Terrace in what is now called Westerwood (the neighborhood didn't have a name when I was growing up). I remember my three-year-old shadow on the sidewalk of Aberdeen Terrace, the giant green parasol that was the fig tree in the backyard. I made my first mud pies there, studded with nandina berries. There was a boy who walked a rabbit on a string. My neighborhood friend Beth Wall and I, playing doctor and nurse one morning at my house, explored our bathroom medicine cabinet and found samples of Digitalis my father had brought home from work (he was a physician, but why did he bring home samples of Digitalis?). Beth and I took the pills, were discovered and rushed to Wesley Long Hospital (then on Elm Street) to have our stomachs pumped. I remember the nurse (who kept asking me to tell her the story of "Goldilocks and the Three Bears" to distract me from the black garden hose they were sliding down my gullet to flush out the poison) telling me that my friend had been much braver during the procedure and didn't I want to be brave like Beth? No, I did not, gagging and sputtering and wailing. Two adults held me down. I thought I would snap like a wishbone. I cared not a hoot for bravery. Bravery was for adults, not children, and I was keen on being a child as long as the privilege lasted. Maybe that was the beginning of my inability or lack of desire to move away from a hometown where I felt comfortable, tended to—albeit violently that morning in the hospital—in spite of my misdemeanors and mistakes. In this case, I eventually felt saved.

Summer 1952. We've moved into a brick ranch house at 3405 Madison Avenue in Starmount Forest. I'm five years old and my brother Knothead is two. My phone number is 8434. I take tap and ballet from Miss Norma, and I have learned shuffle-board-kick. Next year I am going to kindergarten at the Moravian Church on Elam Avenue and my teacher will be Miss Hayworth. I am waiting in the driveway practicing shuffle-board-kick in my shorts and halter top and sandals, while inside the house my mother changes my brother's diaper and outside Daddy loads the car with our suitcases in the hot July sun. He's sweating so hard that his glasses keep sliding down his nose. We are headed to Windy Hill, South Carolina, for our vacation, but I have a terrible secret. I have a ferocious sore throat. I keep pretending every time I swallow that it's only my imagination. But who would imagine a ferocious sore throat if they could imagine better things like the beach? I try to swallow the sore throat down and away. It seems it could work, but it doesn't. I swallow and let thoughts of Windy Hill billow and blow through me until the sore throat is gone with the wind. I've had this kind of sore throat before and it always leads to tongue depressors and Dr. Benbow whooshing out of the exam room in his crackling white coat, and tears hot as blisters leaking from my eyes, and Mother cooing, saying she'll hold my hand, and Dr. Benbow, like Rumpelstiltskin, popping back in with his starchy determined face and a syringe filled with penicillin.

By the time we reach Windy Hill, the sore throat feels like I've swallowed a blazing marshmallow on a stick. I can't eat supper, but I shove food around on my plate so that it looks disturbed by eating. Since I'm a notoriously picky eater, Mother and Daddy don't notice. By morning, the sore throat is dully better, and we go out on the beach. The sand is scalding and the sky bleats light. It hurts my eyes to look, and there's a clang in my head every time I do. Daddy says he liked Nags Head better. Daddy likes everything about North Carolina better. I wish we'd gone to Nags Head, he says, but then goes out to ride his rubber raft on the waves. My brother's diaper is loaded with sand. When he toddles it droops. He sits in a puddle patting the lapping water and laughing. I wish I felt like laughing. Mother's hand feels icy between my shoulder blades, rubbing me with suntan lotion. "Punky, you feel feverish," she says. "Look at me." I look at her and she sees my secret. She always sees my secrets and will read them throughout my life, the ones she really wants to know. But like most mothers, she is selective in her secret-gathering, because what she doesn't know can't hurt her.

Eventually Daddy comes in from riding the big gray waves. She tells Daddy I'm feverish. Back at the hotel, he takes my temperature (he always has his doctor's bag in the car). It's 103 degrees. They give me aspirin and tuck me in. There's lots of murmuring, speculation, sand in the sheets, heat through the open window. The oscillating fan gives me goosebumps. I see blinding tin-roof white whenever I slit my eyes to look at the tilt-a-whirl room. I see an orange peel color when I keep my eyelids closed. I take refuge in the orange peel color. Mother sponges me with a cool washcloth. The fever dips a little, but by evening it's roaring again. Nearly 105, I hear Daddy say. He says I am a furnace. By nightfall I am deep in sleep and don't wake again until we've stopped at an Esso station for gas. We are headed back to Greensboro in the middle of the night. I don't yet know that Daddy is fearful I've come down with polio and Greensboro has means of saving me that Windy Hill does not.

On car trips, whenever we returned to North Carolina, Daddy, like a grateful soldier returning from doing battle in hostile lands, always proclaimed the state motto: "Here's to the land of the long leaf pine, the summer land where the sun doth shine, where the weak grow strong and the strong grow great, here's to down South and the Old North State."

Reciting the motto was as much his travel ritual as eating Chiclets and calling Mother "Navigator," as she kept vigil over the road map open in her lap. Because of Mother we knew where we were going; because of Daddy, we knew we'd get there. I heard the motto through my fever. If Greensboro had had a motto, he would have chanted it upon arriving at its farmy outskirts, for Greensboro was to my father not just the heart of North Carolina but the center of the universe.

I did not have polio, as it turned out. Just a virulent form of strep throat. But this was the height of polio season and Greensboro was in the thick of the epidemic, so much so that in 1948 volunteers built a polio hospital in ninety days to house patients. The hospital, located at East Bessemer Avenue and Huffine Mill Road, remained in operation until 1961 when the polio virus had all but been eradicated.

I suspect that in some peculiar (even pathological) way I have been forever influenced by Daddy's instinct to return to Greensboro. His absolute faith in the healing powers of familiarity, of belonging to a place, lifelong, must have imprinted upon me indelibly. Greensboro as a sanctuary of some sort, capable of saving a child from polio if she had it when Windy Hill could not. Greensboro as a haven from the storms and trials of life. (I often hear people say today that Greensboro has a family-oriented atmosphere, that it's a pleasant place to raise children.) For me, Greensboro has been ines- capable, though there have been times when I've both plotted and longed to be elsewhere, to live somewhere less placid. But, truth to tell, I never tried all that hard to escape. Early in my life I knew I had it good, that I was lucky, that the parents who were in charge of me were kindly shep- herds, not wolves. But later, settling in as the shepherdess in charge of my own lambs, I felt restless. It helped the part of me that lurched toward some undefinable adventure or challenge that I landed a job teaching in the circusy wilds of Chapel Hill. My entire professional life I have been a commuter.

The Greensboro I grew up in was still a small town with aspirations to be bigger. I remember the triumph people felt when the citizenry voted to fund construction of the Greensboro Coliseum so that we wouldn't have to drive to Winston-Salem's coliseum to see the Ice Capades. I-40 never intersnaked its way directly through Greensboro the way it did for years in Winston-Salem, separating the Winston from the Salem. It was as serene and promising a "ribbon of highway" back then as the Woody Guthrie song we sang in our fifth-grade chorus at Sternberger Elementary School. Every time I traveled it as a child, I sang "This land is your land, This land is my land," at the top of my lungs, the wind pummeling me through the rolled-down windows. I-40 was the corridor to the megalopolis that everybody thought they wanted, but that Woody Guthrie would have never endorsed, and would have never sung about.

I have referenced Greensboro in previous writings as "the black hole of niceness" and "the capital of normal," which for a writer is a mixed bag. You need "nice" to get the work done, but you need embroilment in not-nice, too, to write anything with tang. You don't necessarily need to go hunting up trouble; you can find trouble aplenty in what you select to read or hear or observe. In her delicious memoir *Country Girl*, the Irish writer Edna O'Brien observes that writing comes out of "the gouged times, when the heart is cut open." It's what all ex-patriot writers discover, looking back, perhaps, to figure why they left whatever they fled. But there's something else they discover by default: that their places of origin have attached themselves like shadows, following them ever after, no matter where they roam.

That is the nature of growing up anywhere. Our origins pursue us. For any number of reasons, our psyches never fully disengage from the places we come of age. Although one often can't immediately see the wild enchantments of the forest through the cultivated trees and clipped lawns of suburbia, even there the imagination can thrive. The muse abides and incubates, making silk purses out of sows' ears, waiting to declare itself rich when the time is right. We expect art to spring from the riotous, but it can spring from the seemingly plain and normal, too.

We can only tell about a place in any personal and deeply honest way, as we have experienced it. And certainly I have not experienced Greensboro in the way that my dear African American friend Esther Hughes has experienced it. Or the Greens, a brother and sister, who were the first African

American students to attend Grimsley High School when I was a senior there in 1964–65. Or the A&T students who, with trembling decorum, began a revolution with their famous Woolworth's sit-ins in 1960. Or the folks hospitalized at L. Richardson Memorial Hospital, the "black" hospital where my father visited many patients up until its closing. Well into the 1960s, Greensboro's healthcare was segregated.

When I was a child, the least segregated places in Greensboro were the crowded, jostling, homogenizing streets of downtown. My grandfather held on to his hat in the wind. My grandmother clamped on to my hand at the crosswalks, for she sensed me longing to blow away into the gusto of it all. Downtown Greensboro was where all the best shopping was, the cut-rate shoe and jewelry stores, the fancy shops for the well-heeled, like Montaldo's and Younts-DeBoe and Brownhill's. There were three big department stores (one with a tea room) and Schiffman's where people of means bought their wedding rings and china. But also there was South Elm Street, where the scuzzy National Theatre showed monster movies and where the bums slept covered in newspapers near the railroad tracks around Hamburger Square. I understood early that downtown was where the gaudy, exciting tumult was, and as a little girl I hungered for its color and pungency, away from my tidy beige world.

Roaming the sidewalk in front of Ellis-Stone Department Store was scary Mr. Peanut: tall, behatted, with his probing monocle eye, and twirling cane. On Memorial Day my grandmother and I put on our church clothes (you always dressed up to go downtown in those days) and stood on a corner giving out red paper poppies in honor of fallen soldiers, and I observed all sorts of fascinating people who let me in on a bigger whiz bang world than what I knew: a beggar who had no legs and scooted around on a homemade platform with four wheels; the exotic Shriners in their fezzes and ballooning gauzy pants, blowing horns that tooted cobra tunes; rough men in T-shirts, spitting on the sidewalk; white and pink people, brown and black people; once I saw a woman whose skin was polka-dotted white *and* black, no kidding! There were flocks of pigeons making a hullabaloo, and the air smelled of Cracker Jacks.

From third grade on, I was allowed to catch the city bus that stopped at the maple tree on the corner of Madison Avenue and Beverly Place and ride downtown, unchaperoned. The bus let me off in front of the stately courthouse. One bus driver reprimanded me for choosing to sit in the back of the bus. I hadn't a clue why I wasn't allowed to sit there, and the driver never said.

I was innocent for a very long time. My version of Greensboro allowed me to be, whereas others were not so protected. I'm not entirely sure whether long innocence is a good thing. It's probably not. Except that while it shelters, it keeps bitterness at bay. Bitterness obstructs one's vision as much as rose-colored glasses. The inquisitive mind and heart won't tolerate it for long nor forgive an entrenched naiveté.

After the implosions of the majestic King Cotton Hotel and the original O. Henry Hotel, suddenly Greensboro sat under too much sky. Maybe that inspired advancements at the airport. I recall vividly little two-bit Friendship Airport, located at the end of Friendly Road, which threaded its slim two lanes west. Once you passed Westridge Road, there was nothing but farmland, pastoral Guilford College, the fish camp restaurant that overlooked a lake, and cows. Although you walked out on the tarmac to board any plane until the modernized terminal opened in the late 1950s, Friendship Airport always had glamour. One of its earliest modifications was a restaurant where townsfolk often went for special occasions and an outdoor observatory from which you could watch planes take off and land.

Greensboro used to be greener, and that's probably all I need to say about that. But that brings me back to Nathanael Greene, for whom the city is named.

Once my friend Taffy Winston and I were riding our horses in Guilford Courthouse Park (we rode them from the barn on Westridge Road, across Battleground to Lawndale, and entered the park—all this was quite negotiable if marginally safe because in the early 1960s these roads were all two-lane and there wasn't the rush of cars there is today).

Our goal was to hunt out General Nathanael Greene's statue (he's mounted upon an intrepid warhorse) and pay tribute. After all, his preferred mode of transport was equine, same as ours. I don't really remember why we wanted to pay tribute, but it may have had something to do with being required to study North Carolina history in seventh grade. We'd recently read about General Greene and now knew why the town bore his name.

It was fun to go riding with a significant destination in mind. It gave us a kind of cowgirl bravado like we were Pony Express, and it inflated our sense of mission. But here came a uniformed park ranger, big and official as Smokey the Bear, loping over to where we'd dismounted and stood gazing with admiration upon the colossal statue of general and horse. The ranger tipped his hat, then, perhaps sensing we might be troublemakers, sternly informed us that we were not allowed to ride our horses in the park. We were dumbfounded. Where were the signs, huh? We didn't see any signs, we argued. Look! we cried, pointing to General Greene. He rode a horse here!

That was then and this is now, the ranger said. Which is, alas, the caveat of any history lesson.

But enough about my version of Greensboro. All readers of *27 Views of Greensboro* will have their own, and if you've never thought about what Greensboro means to you, this book might jumpstart your own reckoning. So, drumroll, please: Without further ado, here is the book about Greensboro you have been waiting for, in verse and in prose, part personal history, part fact, part fiction, part reminiscence, part advocacy, part deconstruction, part inquisition, part celebration. In delightfully variant voices, these twenty-seven writers deliver a chorus of resonant impressions, reflections, insights, and clear-eyed truths about Greensboro as they have known it. It's quite possible that *27 Views of Greensboro* will answer every question you've ever had about this town but were too busy living the scene yourself to ask. Enjoy!

Marianne Gingher
Spring 2015

MARIANNE GINGHER is the author of the novel *Bobby Rex's Greatest Hit* (which was made into an NBC movie), many short stories, and two memoirs, including *A Girl's Life*, about growing up in Greensboro. Her most recent book, for which she served as editor, is *Amazing Place: What North Carolina Means to Writers*. She is co-founder of Jabberbox Puppet Theater, a Greensboro-based venue for puppetry arts, and is currently Bowman and Gordon Gray Professor of Creative Writing at University of North Carolina at Chapel Hill, where she has taught for many years.

Changing Views

Beyond the Limits of the City

MICHAEL PARKER

THE STUDY OF DENDROCHRONOLOGY allows us to date a tree by counting its growth rings. Those of us who have lived in Greensboro for a while (and I have lived here for twenty-two years, twice as long as I have lived anywhere else) date ourselves by ticking off how many Harris Teeters we have patronized as the grocery store migrates slowly westward up Friendly Avenue. Three different Teeters for me. I have pledged to be long gone from this earth by the time the H.T. reaches Guilford College, but I would not be surprised if, in my lifetime, an even more mega Teeter—one selling yard art and automobile insurance—pops up by the stoplight at Holden Road.[1]

The Harris Teeter has constituted the bulk of my social life. I have gone months without laying eyes on my across-the-street neighbors only to run into them in the pharmacy aisle of the H.T. I see my colleagues from the creative writing program at UNCG as often in the produce section as I do in the halls of academe. In fact, most of our business is conducted there. None of us particularly care for scheduled meetings, but we will cheerfully argue over programmatic particulars while leaning on our half-filled carts.

---

[1] The second incarnation of the Harris Teeter was so grand in its design that some clever resident nicknamed it the "Taj Mah Teeter," a name that quickly stuck.

Grocery stores might be useful to geographers, ethnographers, and students of all things Greensboro in a study of both class and shifting demographics. The arrival of a Whole Foods franchise in Friendly Center meant that Greensboro had proved itself a place where a significant segment of the population could afford to pay three dollars for an avocado. Way out Market Street at the Super G Mart, the produce is decidedly cheaper and far more varied.[2] The Super G is proof of the city's growing international community. Thanks to the presence of the now-defunct Lutheran Family Services, which relocated over 10,000 refugees from such places as Vietnam, Yugoslavia, and the Sudan, the city is no longer primarily black, white, and Native American.[3]

34

In 1938, the historian and sociologist Lewis Mumford predicted the imminent decline of American cities, likening our future to Occupied Europe and equating fascism with the American dependence on "the motorcar." Mumford singled out Greensboro as a cautionary tale, referring to it as "The City of Parking Lots." Greensboroians do love to drive. Virtually no one *walks* to the Harris Teeter, and public transportation, while greatly improved, is not as utilized as in other cities of our size. Because I am cursed with a pathological running habit, I have spent years pounding the paved-over parts of the city, and I rarely have to share the sidewalk.

Though from the start I found Greensboro easily navigable by car, it took me years to figure out why I should get on Wendover Avenue. I realized its allure was the absence — at least in part — of stoplights, but it took a lot longer to figure out where it *went*. In time I learned that Wendover Avenue carries motorcars to dealerships that sell motorcars. If you cross I-40 on Wendover, you will encounter a spread of big-box retailers. People say that if you continue past Best Buy and Super Kmart, you will eventually reach High Point. I will have to take their word on that, just as I accept on faith that High Point Road passes through Adams Farm, which

---

[2] If you are searching for taro root, cane root, arrowroot, lotus root, breadfruit, cactus leaf, kabocha pumpkin, peeled split mung bean, or squid tentacles, the Super G has you covered.

[3] Greensboro is home to one of the largest communities of Lumbee Indians outside their native Robeson County.

until recently I thought was one of those concerns where you could pick your own strawberries.

Greensboro, like other Piedmont cities, was a railroad town, its main industries textiles and tobacco. But it is known for other things. Growing up I knew of the Greensboro-based Pilot Life Insurance Company as a sponsor of ACC basketball; every young basketball fan remembers the spiffy commercial featuring a pilot commanding the steering wheel of a storm-tossed ship. Then there is Vicks VapoRub, developed by resident Lunsford Richardson. Richardson first peddled his mentholated ointment out of the former Porter Drug Store, which he bought from the uncle of Greensboro's famous son William Sydney Porter, aka O. Henry. O. Henry was honored in his hometown by a boulevard that, as far as I can determine, is used only by those who live on or just off it, but he has also had two hotels named after him, one long gone and the other tony and thriving.

It doesn't seem to matter that O. Henry, despite being known as the American answer to Guy de Maupassant, was, like a disproportionate number of writers, a drunk and a thief. Greensboro has always had a colorful side. For years, the main route to downtown from I-40, Lee Street, was a sleazy strip of "oriental" massage parlors and the stray porn shop. The city has long since cleaned Lee Street up, but if you have been here for years, it's hard to come in off the interstate without remembering the flashing neon in the barred windows of the adult businesses. Greensboro has had its share of controversy, both positive—the Woolworth's sit-ins, for which most outsiders know our city—and negative: the 1979 Klan/Nazi shootout with the Communist Workers' Party, which took place at Morningside Homes in east Greensboro and left five protestors dead. It is fitting that Greensboro is known for both a triumphant defiance of Jim Crow and a catastrophic conflagration with the Ku Klux Klan, for like other cities of its size in the South and elsewhere, Greensboro has both made strides in racial equality and still has much work to do.

My favorite place in Greensboro is not technically in the city, but just north of it. The Greensboro watershed trail system contains forty miles of single track hiking, biking, and running trails, much of it on the banks of lakes Brandt, Townsend, and Higgins. When my body can no longer take the pavement of the city of parking lots, I head out to the hilly, root-ruptured trails that snake between Bur Mil and Bryan parks. On many the fall morning, tree leaves still dripping dew, spider webs spun across the paths, I have run for an hour or more without encountering another human being. So wonderfully secluded and peaceful are those trails that I hesitate to include mention of them in this essay, though, like much of what is discussed here, to the true Greensboroian, the trails are no great secret.

I am not, and will never be, a true Greensborian. Though I was born just thirty miles south, I do not identify as a Piedmont-ian. My formative years were spent in the swamps and tobacco fields of Sampson County. Around Greensboro natives I will always feel like a tourist.

To describe a place with authority, the novelist Graham Greene is rumored to have said, you need to have been there less than two weeks or longer than two years. Having exceeded the maximum time period Greene suggests is necessary to truly know a place by two decades, you would think that I could write about Greensboro with some degree of confidence, if not accuracy. But a fiction writer's attitude toward place is complicated by the fact that the worlds we write about are mostly made up; amalgams, perhaps, of real places, but imbued with details — and a prevailing mood — that suit story, not verifiable fact. We are not reporters. Until now, I have never written a word about Greensboro, or set as much as a scene here, but that does not mean it has not altered how I see the world and how I write about what I've seen. The places I write about are, like Greensboro, changing as they stay the same. And in those places, as in Greensboro, the truth is found in the footnotes, the overlooked periphery, the dense and largely untrammeled forests just beyond the limits of the city.

MICHAEL PARKER is the author of six novels and two collections of short fiction. His nonfiction has appeared in the *New York Times*, the *Washington Post*, the *Oxford American*, *Men's Journal*, *Our State*, and *Runner's World*. He is the recipient of a Pushcart Prize, two O. Henry awards, a National Endowment for the Arts fellowship, and the North Carolina Award for Literature. He teaches literature and creative writing at the University of North Carolina at Greensboro.

Our House Has Two Stories

ALLEN JOHNSON

A BIG, SMILING MAN with closely cropped brown hair greeted us warmly as he showed us his home.

There was a living room with a thick, soft green shag carpet. A den with wood-paneled walls. And a big, shady backyard with a concrete patio enclosing the slim, twisting trunk of a dogwood tree that seemed to pirouette in place.

My bedroom-to-be, which I was to share with my baby brother, had built-in shelves where we could display our model ships and planes.

Our kind hosts were the Thompsons. And this was his small but pretty red-brick home in what were then the suburbs off Phillips Avenue.

And they were selling it to us because they were white and we were black and they didn't want to live in a place where black people were moving in. We knew it and they knew it, too. But they seemed to be such decent folks.

The community was called Woodmere Park, and in 1967 and part of 1968, it was a busy runway for white flight—one of the first and most dramatic cases of a white neighborhood turning black in Greensboro, seemingly overnight.

The northeast Greensboro subdivision of 198 homes had been built by developer Joe Koury between 1958 and 1961 and was an entrée into the middle class for working families.

The day we met the Thompsons had come to mind recently because of an odd coincidence. A reader had called me at the newspaper about his letter to the editor, and we struck up a conversation. Turned out we're both from Greensboro and grew up around the same time. He went to Page High School and I attended Dudley. Even though I'd actually lived in the Page High district, I had been allowed to remain at Dudley during desegregation as a "hardship transfer." Dudley had Junior ROTC; Page didn't. That only provoked more questions:

So where did you grow up? he asked.

Woodmere Park, I said.

On what street?

Weyland Drive.

What address?

Nineteen-oh-eight.

There was a sudden, awkward pause.

Allen Johnson meet John P. Thompson, the only child of Nancy and J.P. Thompson.

The perfect stranger who grew up in the same house as you.

We exchanged broad smiles over the phone and immediately began to compare notes: the closet door his dad had sawed in half to clear space for a "built-in" TV in the den; the clear view of the red blinking eye of the Channel 2 tower from the front yard; the quiet old woman who lived behind us and who, as far as I know, was the only white resident who never left Woodmere—until the day she died. Her name was Mrs. Wolfe, John told me.

We later met for lunch at Liberty Oak Restaurant. John, who looks a lot like his dad, shared old Polaroids from his childhood. In one John knelt in a three-point stance in a peewee football uniform. Barely visible in the background was a *For Sale* sign in a neighbor's yard.

For two people who were meeting face to face for the first time, John and I felt a strange sense of familiarity. And we had to laugh when the Crosby, Stills & Nash song "Our House" suddenly began to play in the restaurant. Yet John also confessed a sense of gnawing guilt. "I wish they could have responded to that challenge in a different way," he said of his parents.

But that was a different time and place. We were different.

Not that it didn't hurt to see people flee from us as if we were radioactive.

I recalled one white neighbor who saved her first words to us, and her first smile, for the day she was moving out. A trio of white kids who held two snarling dogs on leashes as we passed and seemed to grin at the prospect of letting them loose. The toddler who playfully called us niggers one day as we walked home from a school bus stop. The whites in passing cars who would taunt us.

But the worst may have been the Duke Power Transit bus driver and white female passenger who one day discussed, matter-of-factly, in front of a half-dozen black people on board how nice Woodmere had been "until the coloreds moved in." As the bus cruised along Woodbriar Drive toward my house, they had not a care for the others. We may as well not have been there.

John Thompson, who was nine years old at the time (I was eleven), recalled his parents' sudden decision to move, quickly, as playing out with minimal explanation to their son.

"They never sat down and said we're moving because black people are coming. . . . I remember a kind of fear on the part of my parents and the folks in my neighborhood. . . . It was like a wave from the ocean that was coming toward us."

John also recognized the harsh illogic at play—that one of his teachers was also one of his first black neighbors in Woodmere. He wondered if that man ever thought to himself that this must mean he was good enough to teach white children but not quite good enough to live near them.

The late J.P. Thompson was an educator as well. He taught shop at Jackson Junior High and driver's ed at Page. The late Nancy Thompson was the first secretary for the Atlantic Coast Conference, where she worked for forty-plus years. His parents sold the house at a loss, John says. After selling their house to us, they moved into an apartment for a while. Then in with relatives. John, his mom, and his dad would sometimes visit Woodmere during Sunday drives.

I liked Woodmere as much as they did. The houses were only slightly larger than in my old neighborhood, but there were trees everywhere. And only a couple of blocks away was a strip shopping center with a 7-Eleven, a pharmacy, and a game center with pinball machines. But I also longed for my old southeast Greensboro neighborhood, Lincoln Heights. So my dad would drop me and my brother off to play there on some Saturday afternoons.

Finally, I recalled my own prejudices—how, years later, my family and I opposed the construction of the Claremont Courts public housing next to Woodmere in the 1970s for fear of the kind of people it would attract and the impact it would have on property values. Today, I would like to think that John and I—and the rest of Greensboro—are older and wiser. More neighborhoods, such as my own, are racially mixed. And the appearance of one or even two black families doesn't ignite the fevered white exoduses that it did in the 1960s.

Yet we are still a largely segregated community. Our schools are even more segregated than in the 1970s. Creeping poverty is creating new race and class divides.

Woodmere today is still a black neighborhood with many well-kept lawns. Rather than buy bigger houses, many residents chose to stay and build additions to their homes, my parents included. One enterprising homeowner wrote a $60,000 check to buy, refurbish, and reopen the historic Proximity Cemetery behind his house.

But Woodmere has a harder edge today. There are more rental properties. The 7-Eleven and pharmacy are long gone, as well as a grocery store that was within walking distance on Phillips Avenue. People in the area have tried for fifteen years to lure a new grocer. They're still trying.

As for John Thompson, whose house my mom still lives in, his honesty and his earnestness make him easy to like.

He met my mother last week at the old house and asked her to forgive him. No need for that, she said. And we shared more pictures and traded more stories about the old neighborhood.

I'm glad I met John Thompson and can call him a new friend.

Even if it took us forty-six years.

Greensboro native **ALLEN JOHNSON** is editorial page editor of the *News & Record*, where a form of this essay first appeared as a column in the newspaper. He and John Thompson have stayed in touch since their chance meeting.

The Bad Old Days

DREW PERRY

You probably won't even need an air conditioner, somebody said. Summer, 1997. *Put a box fan on one end blowing out. Put another on the other end blowing in.*

I'd just moved to Greensboro from Boston. My ex-girlfriend and I had spent the better part of the previous year proving to each other that we ought to stay ex-ed. I had a brand-new pound dog. I'd come for the MFA program, to try to learn how to write. This was my first time living alone. I'd found a one-bedroom shotgun apartment in a hundred-year-old Victorian. I was in a delicate place, is what I'm wanting to say.

I held out maybe a week. But it turns out nobody else could live AC-free, either.

Most of us grad students were living in the same kinds of places, all these apartments cut into all these houses in the same few mainly historical blocks. No one could afford more than one window unit, and no fuse box could survive it, anyway; so the question was this: Do I want to live comfortably during my waking hours, or do I want to sleep at night? Everyone I knew opted for sleep. Set up an air conditioner in your bedroom, close the door a couple of hours before you intend to go in there, suffer through the rest of your apartment growing stiller, smaller—or crank up that box fan—and there is no joy truer than opening the bedroom door and feeling the refrigerator rush of cold air, the growing suspicion that if you work at it hard enough, you might achieve a small thunderstorm in the hallway where the two air masses meet.

Except for sleeping, we lived on front porches.

It was like this for two or three summers. Or six. It's all a wash. We call them the bad old days now. We were poor. We were happy. Mornings we wrote, or worked odd jobs. We survived until the afternoon. We had baby pools in the front yards. One fairly sodden string of weeks, I am ashamed to admit, we bleached those pools to keep them from turning green—it was hard work, the dumping and refilling, and the water bills grew expensive. I had a buddy who dug a full pond, waist-deep, into the yard behind his apartment. Another who hung a junker window unit off his porch railing, extension cord running around the side of the house, coolish air blowing out the front, blast furnace out the back. We kept what beer we could afford—so off-brand we had to special-order it from the grocery store—on ice in broken coolers. We had plans to affix lawnmower wheels to one of the dead refrigerators in somebody's basement and make a sort of soapbox derby car, but no one could figure out a suitable braking system. When it rained—if it ever rained—we'd set up two-liter soda bottles in the street, pull an actual bowling ball from a tractor-tire flowerbed, and bowl, mid-storm, right down the middle of the road. Three separate people had to serve as backstops—we were worried the ball would roll through the intersection and maim somebody, or worse.

The neighborhood association loved us.

Summer is for children, and that's what we were. We were too old for it, and knew it. Or we knew that we were almost too old, and were spending those years trying everything we could to hang on. To keep whatever was coming at bay. And now it's here. We're grown. We're married. We have jobs, functioning automobiles, clean laundry, central air—some of us may even, though I shudder to think of it, be members of neighborhood associations.

I have two boys. A bunch of us have children. Those of us who are still here get together on summer weekends, cook out in the backyard, let the kids chase each other through sprinklers. And while that's summer through and through—fireflies, watermelon, kids right up against the edge of injury—we try not to forget the old summers altogether. Last year a friend down the street, a veteran of those bad old days, rock-salted a cooler, froze everything inside. He was thrilled. We all were. And while the kids played, while we watched them, we set in right away trying to improve his system, trying to figure out how to do it right.

Still here. That's the thing. I was supposed to have to leave. We all were. And some of us did, I guess, though a lot of those folks left and came back. Greensboro is a place absent an obvious geographical feature—no hill, no water—but something here takes hold. Maybe it's the trains I'm having to explain to my older son now, the trains you can hear all over the city, all evening long. Or maybe it's the fireworks. I've never lived anywhere with a higher frequency of pyrotechnics. Maybe it's the remaining complement of seasons—Greensboro puts on a solid autumn, a lovely winter, freezes the blossoms off the trees mid-March with near-clockwork precision. Or maybe all of that is wash and spume, and it's the summer, after all: The still, dry brutality of August; the lone long-sleeve day each early June that, pre-kids, used to lend itself to all-day front porch reading; the hometown minor league baseball and the several other teams within an hour's drive. Now, we walk to dinner parties, diaper bag and casserole both slung beneath the stroller. We mow the lawn once the sun drops behind the trees. We discuss at extraordinary length possible ways of preventing or at least delaying Yellow Death, the catchall phrase for the host of diseases that kill off our tomatoes every year. We grill—all foods, in all weathers. Listen to the cicadas. Drop ice in the glass. Keep the kids up late, and then put them mercifully to bed.

Someone recently asked me what my hometown was, and I was a sentence or two into explaining that it was Atlanta, that I'm from Atlanta, before it dawned on me: I'm not. Not really. Not any more. I got baptized in those bad old days. Survived the baby pools. Came out the other side brand new. I could never have imagined that we'd stay, that from that would come a marriage, a family, a life. This house, this street. These summers. This town. Or maybe that's not quite it, either. Maybe it's this: Once here, I could never imagine anything else.

DREW PERRY is the author of *Kids These Days* and *This Is Just Exactly Like You*. A portion of this essay first appeared in *O.Henry* magazine.

Sayf[1]

DIYA ABDO

Summer 2008

I do not want to leave Jordan.

My departure will be a self-imposed exile.

The previous summer, I had returned from whitewashed rooms carved into sloping mountains atop the bluegreen waters of Santorini to an email with a foreboding, though ambiguous, title: *Official Notification*. I could not have imagined that it contained in its belly the Arab and Muslim woman academic's death blow.

> Dear Dr. Diya Abdo,
>
> I have been asked by the Director of the Jordan Branch to inform you to submit your resignation as your publications and ideas are unacceptable at Arab Open University and are not in accordance with Arab Islamic values, which are an essential part of this institution's philosophy and mission. Your emphasis on queer theory, sexual fluidity and attack on Arab/Islamic culture and values are in direct opposition to the philosophy of this institution. Thus, in order to avoid action being taken against you at Headquarters in Kuwait, we are asking you to submit your resignation as soon as possible.

---

[1] "Summer" in Arabic.

I rail, then challenge, then placate; they finally recant. But it's too late—I feel betrayed, soured, dirtied. I bide my time, scour the job ads, and finally find 6,000 miles away the Guilford job. I tell my recommendation-letter writers: "This is the one."

When Guilford flies me in for the interview, it is my first time in North Carolina. Jim Hood, then chair of the English department, meets me at the airport. I already know what he looks like from his photo online, and somehow, he recognizes me too. His face is beaming, and we are joking with each other from the very first minute; instantly, we are like sister and brother.

But on the way to Guilford, driving through undeveloped land, my stomach drops. And it hits me that after Amman International Airport and JFK, the GSO airport seems more like a bus stop. I am an Arab city woman; I am at home in the suffocating exhaust of public buses and exhausted cars, the heat rising in visible waves off the baking asphalt, the constant hum and drone of shopkeepers inviting you into their stores, and perhaps most unshakably, the muezzin's call to prayer, rising slowly, and then wailing triumphantly, several times a day.

For months after I settle in Greensboro, I still hear it at the appointed time—the phantom *azan* calling from the distance, the recesses of my mind unable to let go of this primordial sound imprinted in me in utero.

Summer 2009

Aidana Sabha is born. She is my first daughter, conceived while my grand-mother, Sabha, the woman who raised me, lay dying in the hospital. For years, she had been urging me to have a child. When I left Jordan, it broke her heart. I didn't know how to tell her about the death blow. (Did she think I wanted to leave her?) They took her to the hospital a week after I left; she never returned to Palestine like she always dreamed. On the phone: "Teita, I am pregnant." From her hospital bed: "Mabrouk, ya Dthiya', mabrouk ya habibti" (*Congratulations, Diya. Congratulations, my love*). The next day she died—on my birthday. The autopsy revealed a cancer, undetected and voracious; starving, it had consumed her liver.

At the parks, I observe the other parents with their kids. I unconsciously try to be like the parents at my favorite haunt, Lake Daniel Park, which is lovely and shaded. There are toys in abundance in the sandbox, left there by the keepers of growing children who no longer have need of them. Watchful and patient, the white, middle-class mothers and fathers center their outings around their children. They are a picture of organization. I keep a tally in my mind of how many times I hear the phrase: "It's 5:30. You can play for five more minutes and then we have to leave to fix supper."

But "my people" are elsewhere; they go to parks like the one at the end of the arboretum (though I rarely see them in the arboretum itself). There are no toys there, and the women talk among themselves; the children play alone or, most often, together. They are loved, but they are not the only. The families stay until dusk, and maybe even beyond. Dinner is whenever they get home. Occasionally, a woman yells at her child to come back from the edge of the river or stop throwing rocks at the mulberry.

The white parents walk up to their children, bend down, insist on making eye contact and, with a firm hand on a petulant shoulder, calmly and rationally negotiate a reprimand in hushed tones. Not embarrassing the child is paramount.

The brown kids are always, and so never, embarrassed.

I feel comfortable here but for now, I still act like the Lake Daniel Park parents except for the one thing on which I will never compromise: Arabic. From the day Aidana is born, I speak with her only in Arabic, and I expect her to do the same with me. I am deaf to her English.

This is non-negotiable. Language is identity, and hers must be, will be, Arab.

In a swing at Lake Daniel Park, I am chattering to Aidana in Arabic. A white woman is cooing with her child in the next swing. He becomes upset. She says, "Are you scared because you don't understand what they are saying?" She takes him out of the swing to play elsewhere. Thankfully, there are not many moments like this.

Summer 2012

Something remarkable happens. I have been in Jordan for ten days, too short a time to be sure, and am about to board the plane that, thirteen hours later, will land me at JFK. Now this has happened *many* times before—too many to count. *Every* time, this has been a moment of deep despair. Jordan is home, so how could it not be? Except this time. As I carry my sleeping three-year-old daughter, and walk the length of that dank tunnel on this hot day in July, I feel immensely happy to have come back home to Jordan to visit and immensely happy to be going back home to Greensboro to live. For someone who has always felt unhomed, having two homes means that, this time, I won't have to sob hopelessly and silently as the female airport security officer outlines my body with her scanner; the easting desert sun will be there, westing upon my arrival.[2]

Summer 2013

Miraculously, my sister has moved to Greensboro to pursue a graduate degree. She has two daughters, one the age of my daughter and one two years older. They live at the Legacy Apartments which we call "Saudi Central"—there are no less than twenty Saudi families living there. Starbucks, less than half a mile away, is "Sudan Central."

How can it be that in a place as small as Greensboro, there are so many of us?

If I crave the obscurest of Arab delicacies (like *hamleh* or *loz akhdar*), I find it at the Super G Mart. The Asian cashiers have no idea how we eat or use them; they've asked us several times at checkout. If my sister needs the choicest halal meat for her *mensef*, she finds it at El-Baraka Market

---

2 "Easting" and "westing"—literal translations of the Arabic for "sunrise" and "sunset."

on Patterson. If I want spices for my *hara' usba'o* or *shorbet adas,* I drive the two minutes to Al-Madina Market. If I long for an honest-to-goodness falafel sandwich, I drive to Jerusalem Market on Highpoint Road and get to chat with the owner Ammo Salibah to boot. Once, he tells me, a man walked into his shop and asked him how long he'd been a Christian. "For two thousand years," Salibah replied.

Summer 2014

From the land of fig and olive groves, by way of the desert, to me all green is precious.

When I first came to Greensboro, I couldn't tell the trees from each other. A willow oak looked like a weeping cherry looked like a gumball looked like a dogwood; and I definitely couldn't tell the weeds from the flowers from the poison ivy. Jim Hood tells me to cut the English ivy back. It snakes over the fences and steals around the deck, its tendrils slithering between its cracks. It will ruin the wood, he says. But Jim and his wife, Sara Beth, are self-admitted "tree snobs"; they want to cut down the Bradford pears in their front yard.

I am sad for days when, digging a pond in the back yard, my husband cuts away at the roots of the crabapple that shades the back deck. This tree is more than a nuisance; it's actively destructive. Every fall, the small, gnarly apples, mushy and grainy, *thud thud thud* on our aging deck. They squish underfoot and the deck turns into a killing field of orange-red apples, their guts splattered everywhere, the odor of deep rot rising from the planks. My husband wouldn't mind if his hacking away has killed it; he wants something else in its place anyway, and that's sensible. But I can't imagine cutting down a living tree; all green is precious, even when it yields messy rot every November.

It seems we won't know if he's killed it for another year or so. I wait, not knowing whether the tree is on death row. In the meantime, the chipmunks living under the deck, the ones not slaughtered by our one-eyed

Jordanian cat, will still be able to sit, in moments of stolen safety, on the steps nibbling away at the little fruit, leaving behind a small pile of leftovers as a testament to their presence.

At "Saudi Central," we've settled into a life that reminds me of the streets of Jordan. Seira Emer is eight months old. The older girls play outside with the hordes of Saudi kids, their fathers drinking coffee and chatting well into the night on woven plastic mats. The fathers have got plenty of ice cream for all the kids who might be playing outside and hand them out whenever a child, sugar-crazed (like my niece Alana) or stranger-shy (like my daughter Aidana), asks for one. They don't check with us whether "it's okay to give her ice cream?" The Lake Daniel Park parents would not have ice cream and would *never* hand it out to asking kids. The Saudi women sit on the iron table next to the small park, shelling watermelon and pumpkin seeds, drinking Saudi coffee, and fiddling with their iPhones. I sit with my sister on the stoop of her apartment overlooking the park, swatting away the flies, my generous thighs feeling the warmth of the brick under me, keeping a distant eye on Aidana. I rest Seira in the bend of my arm, elbow digging into the soft spot above my knee, legs as far apart as possible, and nurse her. Occasionally, I yell at Aidana to watch out as the kids weave in and out of the men playing volleyball in the sand. It pleases me to think that my grandmother would have done it just like this—squatting on the ground under the olive trees, gossiping with other women, a baby on the breast, and a child playing in the groves. But this isn't Jabal Al-Mukabber. Aidana wants long, blonde hair like Elsa, the Icelandic Ice Queen, and tomorrow, I will go to Guilford and teach American kids how to write in English and how to analyze literature in English, and I might go to Whole Foods to pick up what I can afford of their mock chicken poppy salad.

But for now, I sit in the sun and nurse Seira the way a Palestinian village woman would.

DIYA ABDO is a first-generation Palestinian, born and raised in Jordan. Currently an associate professor of English and chair of the English department at Guilford College, she teaches and writes about Arab women writers and Arab and Islamic feminisms. She loves hanging out with her daughters in Greensboro's beautiful parks and eating in the city's many excellent restaurants. While she has many academic publications, this is her first piece of creative nonfiction.

Sweet Magnolia

LOGIE MEACHUM

MY BROTHER LARRY AND I caught the 10 Walker Avenue bus to go to school every day. We grew up in the Woodyside community, a rural, all-black neighborhood located just a mile or two from the front gates of Guilford College. If you drove to Guilford from our house, you would pass an elementary, middle, and high school, but we could not go to any of those schools in 1960. We went to school thirteen miles away on the black side of Greensboro. My father's Aunt Joe lived across the street from a school in that neighborhood, so that was where we went. My father or mother took us every morning several miles past our local schools to Muirs Chapel Road where we caught the city bus. That bus then took us to Our Lady of the Miraculous Medal School in the middle of the largest black community in the city of Greensboro. At that time, it was a community; today, it is a neighborhood with all that comes with "hoods."

We waited each morning for the bus on Muirs Chapel Road in the driveway of a little, old white lady's house. Her name was Mrs. Bray. (Years later during integration, her grandson and I became very good friends and remain friends unto this day.) It was usually dark when we were dropped off at Mrs. Bray's, and we waited inside her house on those cold winter mornings. Even though my mother had fed us breakfast, Mrs. Bray invited us to sit at her kitchen table and eat her apple butter toast. It was a treat, so we never turned her down. I loved that. At seven o'clock or so, the bus would stop beneath the big oak tree in her yard.

From Muirs Chapel we went east on Market Street, to United Street, to Holden Road, and onto Walker Avenue, passing Woman's College (now UNCG) and into downtown Greensboro to the Morris and Neese Furniture Company on Green Street where the Jim Melvin Plaza is today. There, young black men with brick mason's bags, kids going to school, and lots of swollen-ankled, older black women gathered, waiting to catch a bus to the white side of town to take care of families before returning home to their own latchkey kids on the five o'clock bus.

At Morris and Neese, we usually had to wait a few minutes to transfer to another bus. I saw a lot of the world there—the A&T students marching and the sit-ins going on at Woolworth's. Once the No. 5 Gorrell Street bus delivered us to the black side of town, we could run amok on the A&T campus, smell hair frying, hear the sound of gospel music from WEAL, and feel the heartbeat of a community on the move. John Kennedy was president during some of that period, and at the Catholic school we attended the nuns had us pray for him every day. President Kennedy and Dr. Martin Luther King Jr. were all folks talked about. Black folk were excited; you could feel it in the air, as strong as the emotion and spark that permeated the community during A&T homecoming or revival season in the local black churches.

The No. 5 Gorrell Street bus went under the bridge at Market Street and Murrow Boulevard, which was and remains the gateway to the soul side of town. As we headed toward Gorrell Street, my mind focused on two special places: Fire Station No. 4 had Greensboro's only all-black crew, who to me and other kids at the time were local heroes; the other site was the Magnolia Hotel.

There were lots of goings-on in Greensboro during the early 1960s, but nothing was as exciting to me as riding the No. 5 bus past the Magnolia

Hotel, because every day the marquee in its front lawn announced who was residing within its walls for the evening. *Staying Here Tonight*, the sign said, *Charlie and Inez Foxx*, or maybe *Ike and Tina Turner*. Sometimes it read *Ray Charles*, or *Sister Rosetta Tharpe, James Brown, Little Richard*. A host of stars came and went at the Magnolia, either while they were performing at the El Rocco Supper Club in the city or just traveling from the more open North to the segregated South where few hotels were available to them. The Magnolia was a known safety zone, even for the more famous and well-known *coloreds*, as we were called in those days.

When the bus passed the Magnolia, I would stare at the hotel and imagine what would possibly happen at a breakfast table with James Brown and the Five Blind Boys of Alabama. Did Mahalia Jackson take over the kitchen while she was there? Why did Charlie and Inez Foxx stay there when they were from Greensboro? Must have been the cooking. The Gist family who ran the Magnolia had access to all the famous *colored* acts of the day and I envied everything about their proximity to those folks I thought were God's angels on earth. I listened to their songs at my grandfather's corner store where we dropped nickels and dimes into what we called a "piccolo" and other folks called a jukebox. On Saturdays I listened to the latest tunes on 45s in the Chavis Handy Corner, danced until I couldn't find a dry spot on my clothes, and then, on the way to school on Monday, stared wide-eyed when I passed the Magnolia in hopes of seeing any of my heroes who stayed there overnight.

Often, after school I could go up to Bennett College, also on Gorrell Street, to the Carnegie Negro Library and check out books. I would sit and read and memorize as much as I could of the poetry of Paul Laurence Dunbar. My grandmother recited Dunbar's poetry, as did most of her children. As one of the oldest grandchildren, I couldn't wait to learn Dunbar's poems or "The Creation," by James Weldon Johnson, so that I could recite as we sat around the wood stove the way that my aunts and uncles did whenever there was a snow storm or just on a Sunday when we were all together on the corner of Hibler and Aloe roads in the Woodyside community. While I was at the Carnegie library, I was always tempted to see who was *Staying Here Tonight* at the Magnolia. I'd take a few moments to run across the Bennett College campus and go up to the corner where the Magnolia was and find out. Often there was no word of the famous and fabulous, and I would walk back down Gorrell to my Aunt Joe's house across the street from Miraculous Medal School. I would sit on her front porch or roll down the hill in the grass and dream of that breakfast table in the Magnolia.

Today the Magnolia is under renovation. On occasion, I am hired to come to the Magnolia by a touring company owned by my good friend Dr. Sandra Alexander. When the tour bus pulls up, I hop on and pretend to be the local guitar legend, James "Guitar Slim" Stephens, who in real life happens to be a friend of mine. (I played guitar and spent many a day with Slim drinking Relska Vodka that he kept in the bucket at the bottom of his well.) Dr. Alexander likes my interpretation of Guitar Slim, so I serve as a blast from the past. Even though the Magnolia Hotel has not yet opened, we look at it from the bus. I talk briefly about its history, and then sing a song, recite a poem, and hop off the bus so that they can continue their tour of Greensboro.

Funding for the renovation project has been slow, but the Magnolia looks absolutely grand. I plan to spend a weekend there just as soon as it opens as one of the city's newest bed and breakfast facilities. While I'm there, I will sing James Brown songs and make believe I can hear the Five Blind Boys of Alabama harmonizing on the front porch. I hope to hear Mahalia Jackson loosening her pipes in the upstairs bathroom as if she was preparing to do a show at the Hayes-Taylor YMCA as she did many times in the Sixties. Perhaps Ray Charles will play a piano downstairs in my dream and James Brown will sing "Tell Me What'd I Say" with Ray.

I want to hear Greensboro's own Charlie and Inez Foxx singing "Mockingbird." Yeah, I can't wait. Maybe they will write on the marquee, *Staying Here Tonight: Logie Meachum.* Yeah . . . oh yeah, now that would be a dream come true.

LOGIE MEACHUM is a storyteller, teacher, and blues musician. Raised in the Guilford College/Friendship community, he has always loved stories and the history of his home state in general and the Woodyside neighborhood in particular. He also operates the Old Oak Stump Gardens and is founder of the Second Greater Recreationalist Congregation. "Do what you can for the people. Amen."

Ghost City

EDWARD CONE

ABOUT EIGHT THOUSAND YEARS AGO somebody left an arrowhead in what is now New Irving Park. Maybe its owner shot it at some supper or at another person. Maybe it just got lost. In any case it was there, circa 1947, to be discovered by a Boy Scout camping by Buffalo Lake.

Flash forward another twenty-five years. The now-grown kid brings his own children to the same spot. My sister and I are supposed to be looking for arrowheads, but we are distracted by the bulldozers scraping the woodland bare. An advance guard of the upper-middle class is preparing for the leap north from Brown Town to suburbia's next frontier. This is my first time watching Greensboro devour its landscape at scale.

Engraved above the doorway to the museum of Southern clichés is Faulkner's maxim: "The past is never dead. It's not even past." But chunks of our past keep disappearing. The Panic of 2008 arrested, for a while, the clonal propagation of real estate development across Guilford County. Today you can drive out Bryan Boulevard or Battleground and gaze upon the acreage cleared to make room for a network of big-ass roads, which pretty much guarantee more of the same.

And while the built environment spreads, it eats its own. Decades after the fact, people lament the way Warnersville got urban-redeveloped right off the map, taking a good chunk of African American history—of Greensboro's history—with it. Now UNCG is looking at Glenwood the way a butcher looks at one of those diagrams of a cow with the cuts of beef drawn on it. War memorials tend to come with an expiration date around here. Even unmourned casualties like the massive Sears warehouse on Lawndale take something of value with them, some part of the story of this place.

I know, grow or die. One person's pain is another's progress. The implosion of the Burlington Industries headquarters, a modernist classic on Friendly Road that symbolized the region's economic vitality, was protested at the time by preservationists and other fuddy-duddies (a dwindling few of us even recalled horses roaming the Benjamins' pasture before the glass-and-steel box went up). But most of the crowd cheered as the girders buckled. They enjoyed the show—the same way I did back in grade school when the King Cotton Hotel was erased from the downtown skyline. Now they've got an Apple Store and a Williams-Sonoma.

What gives a place its identity? It's been a while since Greensboro could answer that question. For most of the twentieth century this was a confident town, second-largest in the state, prospering around a cluster of companies with deep local roots and national reach. Globalization, consolidation, and automation took care of that. There was no Plan B. And because the landscape is undramatic, lacking a mountain or river to instantly say "home" to locals across eras, it can feel like there is no there here.

If you were to argue that transience is Greensboro's most enduring trait I would concede that you had a defensible position. Moving on is as much an American habit as overuse of the past tense is a Southern one, and we live them both. The general from whom we borrowed our name was just passing through on a business trip, and favorite son O. Henry, like other celebrated natives in his wake, got out as soon as he could. Our best-known nickname, the Gate City, advertised a rail junction as the "gateway to the

60

South"—thanks for coming, bye-bye. The same value proposition lay behind the huge Overseas Replacement Depot during World War II and the construction of the interstates and an air-freight hub. We brag about our GPS coordinates in terms of proximity to the mountains and the beach, and even the geological designation of *piedmont* is defined by the region next door.

The past persists but it is not (to steal William Gibson's line about the future) evenly distributed. Sometimes it is neatly packaged, like at Blandwood Mansion or the national military park (the fact that our Revolutionary War battlefield was abandoned for a century before being rescued by local boosters shows how changeable our relationship with history can be). It's there in secret spots like an overgrown springhouse from the 1700s on an intact but besieged family farm north of town, and it is part of the present at Buffalo Presbyterian Church on Sixteenth Street, where the original brick building has been a constant since 1827. Look carefully at the worn gravestones in the cemetery and then look up the family names in the telephone directory and you can see human continuity, too.

And there is an oral tradition, kept alive by people who pass along the stories they grew up with. My internal map of Greensboro has overlays of the town as sketched by my father and his parents, with grace notes they learned from more-distant relatives and friends in a shake-the-hand-that-shook-the-hand kind of deal stretching back to Reconstruction. In my inherited memories of things I never saw, there is a ghost city where streetcars run on tracks through a busy downtown, the swells live in big houses on Summit Avenue, and Hamilton Lakes and White Oak are villages unto themselves. It seems real to me, and relevant.

Not everything was better back then (back there?) or worth preserving. Any sentimental view of the past is fiction, and being a ghost city beats being a ghost town. An even older Greensboro than the one my grandfather recalled for me built its fancy homes along Asheboro Street; those folks would have had a collective heart attack if they had lived to see their grand thoroughfare rechristened Martin Luther King Jr. Boulevard.

My wife and I raised our kids in the neighborhood that emerged from the red mud where my dad taught me to look for arrowheads. I was a cheerleader for the downtown performing arts center and hope we will fund the rest of the Urban Loop before I'm too old to drive.

Greensboro's relative decline among North Carolina cities means we have lost less of our old character than the boomtowns we envy. But that is not for want of trying, and it could change with any uptick in our fortunes. I worry that downtown's current growth spurt, the biggest in decades, will have developers eyeing the weathered glory of South Elm Street, and I know the completion of the ring road will doom a nearby horse farm that was treasured by my daughter. Even if we hit the right mark between renewal and replacement, we risk turning this place into someplace else.

EDWARD CONE grew up in Greensboro, where he and his wife, Lisa, raised their two children. For many years he was an opinion columnist for the *News & Record* and a reasonably popular blogger, all while maintaining a career as magazine writer and editor for publications in the wider world.

Fish Store Mural Relocated

MARK SMITH-SOTO

A splash of light on the gray bricks, the mermaid
lounges in a flowing, horizontal pose, her body —
breasts cuddled behind a forearm cross — twisting
so her sleepy eyes sweep the length of Lee Street.
She might have woken up on this block just in time
to see the skinny boy in T-shirt and huge sneakers
pay for a gun in the parking lot, glimpse the wheel-
chaired figure on the corner waving a sign that says
Vet Out of Work, Can Fix Anything. Long she
flourished here, brightening the dilapidated shops,

until the city felt the need to rescue her, brick
by brick, to a more prosperous side of Greensboro.
Her elegant tail, perfectly scaled, no longer waves,
but since the workers haven't reached her head, her
smile's unchanged. And though the coral lipstick's
cracked a bit, there's such an openness in her face
it's no wonder we want to lead her off to a place
untouched by roadside trash, where the homeless
won't huddle under her at night and let their dreams
trouble the quiet tide of her green hair.

MARK SMITH-SOTO has been editor or associate editor of *International Poetry Review* at the University of North Carolina at Greensboro for over twenty years. He has published four prize-winning chapbooks and two poetry collections, *Our Lives Are Rivers* and *Any Second Now*. His work has appeared in *Antioch Review, Kenyon Review, The Sun,* and other journals. His most recent publications are *Berkeley Prelude: A Lyrical Memoir* and the chapbook *Splices.*

Gentrification and its Discontents

Forty Years in Fisher Park

RICHIE ZWEIGENHAFT

WHEN THE REALTOR showed my wife and me the house we now have lived in for forty years, she warned us that the neighborhood, Fisher Park, was "iffy." For instance, there was a car parked on the front lawn of the rental property across the street. We came to conclude that what she really meant was that the house was just a block from the railroad tracks that divide the east side of Greensboro from the west side. Greensboro was even more segregated residentially then than it is now, and many black residents lived just across the tracks, a few blocks from what was to become our house. Definitely *iffy* in realtor-speak.

We loved the house. In fact, we had admired it months earlier while visiting our friend Charlie Trueheart who worked at the local newspaper and lived around the corner. It reminded us of one of our favorite houses in our previous hometown, Santa Cruz, California. Built around 1908, the house had interesting architectural features, one of which was a welcoming front porch. My wife and I each had a list of about ten things we were looking for in a house. Our lists overlapped, though not completely. We both wanted a house and a neighborhood that allowed for what we called *funkiosity*. I had on my list that the house or yard needed to have a place to hang a basketball hoop, but that was not on my wife's list.

When the realtor unlocked the front door and we walked inside, we could see all three fireplaces—one straight ahead, one in the room to the right, and one in the room to the left. We both totally ignored our lists and knew immediately that we wanted to buy it, which we did (long story), and we have never regretted the decision. We think of it as the center of the universe (at least, the center of our universe).

We were pleased to learn that Fisher Park had a neighborhood association, and we attended a meeting, led by a formidable woman (Mary Lee Copeland). It turned out that the neighborhood had organized in order to fight off a number of developers with various projects. For example, the association rose up against an attempt on the part of a group called Greensboro Beautiful to convert the park itself that nestles in the middle of Fisher Park into a formal garden (we won that one, and maybe the entire city won—Greensboro Beautiful subsequently found land near Friendly Shopping Center for what is now called the Bicentennial Garden and the nearby Bog Garden, both of which are great community resources). The neighbors then fought a plan to tear down two beautiful old houses on the corner of Elm Street and North Park Drive and build a high-rise in what is essentially the middle of the neighborhood. The houses were torn down, but instead of a high-rise, some fancy, upscale townhouses were built, a good enough compromise, even if their saltbox design had the roof angled backward from the way real saltboxes look.

At about this time, some residents began to push for the neighborhood to seek historic district status. The neighbors were split. Many, including my wife and me, strongly supported it, hoping that it would protect us from the ever-voracious developers (what the urban sociologists call "the growth machine"). Others, including some of the older neighbors, were against it, fearing bureaucratic governmental control (their fears were increased by some who told them, falsely, that they would never be able to paint their houses or plant a tree without governmental approval). Tempers flared, people argued, tires were slashed, but Fisher Park became a historic district. Property values soared, and gentrification began.

In the first decade that we lived here, we became friends with some of our neighbors. And, much to our delight, a number of our friends who lived in other neighborhoods or who were moving to Greensboro moved into Fisher Park. At one point — now we're talking the mid- to late-1980s — I realized that for the first time since I'd lived in a dorm in college many of my close friends lived within walking distance. After college, when I was in graduate school (first in New York City and then in Santa Cruz), and when I held my first job (in Upstate New York), I had to get in my car or use public transportation in order to see my close friends. Now, however, as had been the case in my increasingly distant undergraduate days, I could walk to see them. Just walking around the block with the dog (dog then, dogs now) could take an hour because we inevitably ran into friends.

Gentrification happened gradually, with periodic jolts of shock on my part ("Gee, a lot of people are adding rooms to their houses!" "Wow, some neighbors now are driving BMWs and Mercedes!" "Jesus, a Jaguar in Fisher Park?!"). Nothing, however, symbolizes the transformation of Fisher Park more than the house of our former neighbor, Mrs. Keaton. Once a factory worker, Mrs. Keaton was an old and cranky woman in 1975 when we moved in, and she was an older, crankier, and much more reclusive woman when she died thirty years later. By the time she died, the neighborhood was well into gentrification, so her house stood out like a sore thumb. It needed a paint job. Almost no upkeep had taken place either inside or out in many years. And the *pièce de rèsistance* was the tattered green awning hanging eerily over the front porch, giving the house a certain Boo Radley look.

After Mrs. Keaton died, the house sat empty for a number of years. Although I knew an empty house "wasn't good for the neighborhood," and many neighbors complained, I kind of liked it. It served as a reminder of those young and adventurous days with that car in the front yard across the street. More to the point, no matter how beat up our picket fence looked (we scrounged it from the side of the road in 1977) or overgrown our shrubs became (the city had told us twice, once in 1990 and again in 2007—repeat offenders!—that we had to trim them so that people had more room to walk by on the sidewalk), there was always Mrs. Keaton's house to show we weren't so bad.

Then an architect and his wife bought Mrs. Keaton's house and put an immense amount of time and money into it. They gutted the inside and did a beautiful job restoring it. They landscaped the front yard. They put elegant cobblestones into the driveway and replaced the old sidewalk with a fancy new brick one. The house became a jewel, and I'm sure the value of our property increased. I, needless to say, had mixed feelings about this.

I can't say we have not contributed to the gentrification of Fisher Park. Old picket fence and overgrown shrubbery and all, we've done a few expansions. First, back in 1981, we added a studio to the back of the house for my wife, a potter. Then, in about 2002, we ponied up for a major remodeling project that created a bigger kitchen and added a downstairs bathroom. In the summer of 2014, we "did" the kitchen again (we resisted the temptation to replace the maple countertops with granite ones like the ones so many of our neighbor friends have added to their remodeled kitchens). Although I still drive a 1995 Toyota that has lacked a hubcap on one wheel for about ten years, my wife, like many of our neighbors, drives a Prius.

We probably have taken cabs two or three times in our forty years in Greensboro. A few years ago, my wife was coming back from the airport in a cab (I was out of town) and she gave the cab driver our address. His reply? "Oh, you're one of those rich folks in Fisher Park." She had to explain to him that we love our neighborhood, but that we had arrived before being rich was a requirement. It did, however, give us a different take on where we live, how we are perceived, and, maybe, who we have become.

RICHIE ZWEIGENHAFT is Charles A. Dana Professor of Psychology at Guilford College and the coauthor of four books, most recently *The New CEOs: Women, African American, Latino, and Asian American Leaders of Fortune 500 Companies.* He is still known to some as Rockaday Johnny from his days in the 1970s and 1980s as a disc jockey on WQFS, and to others as Commish either because of his role as commissioner of the mid-day geezer basketball game at Guilford (a game that began in 1976) or because of his role as commissioner of the Fisher Park Fantasy Baseball League.

A Grave Situation

MARIA JOHNSON

WHERE ARE YOU GOING TO BE BURIED?

It's not a great icebreaker, but the question does cross your mind from time to time, especially as you get older and watch more people pass into the great beyond.

The great below.

Whatever.

My husband and I flitted around the burial question for years, but only recently did we get around to shopping for plots, mainly because my parents, who moved to Greensboro twenty years ago to be closer to us (i.e., their grandchildren), have talked about selling a couple of plots they own in another town and buying plots in Greensboro to be closer to us, you know, in the permanent sense.

After all, unless you're from a family of exhumers, you're usually buried in just one place. It's not like you have a summer plot and a winter plot, or a beach plot and a mountain plot, or even a starter plot and an I've-arrived plot.

You pretty much get one shot at your plot.

So my mother asked where would we want to "be."

Jeff and I narrowed the possibilities to two: Forest Lawn Cemetery and Green Hill Cemetery. Both are operated by the City of Greensboro, which is good because you figure a city will always maintain its cemeteries, plus they give city residents a price break. I like to think of it as a less-festive version of renting a picnic shelter.

The city actually operates three cemeteries—Maplewood is the third—but Forest Lawn and Green Hill are the closest to where we live, which is important because, let's face it, you want it to be convenient for your survivors to bawl their eyes out over your grave.

Not that you want them to be despondent over the loss of you.

Not long-term.

But a tasteful cry now and then would be nice.

Maybe a few apologies.

And a couple of "You were so rights."

You know, basic graveside manners.

We visited Green Hill first.

It was a rainy, dreary morning, and I grappled with the obvious: What to wear while grave shopping? Something comfortable. With sensible shoes. Nothing too upbeat. But nothing too morose either. After all, we weren't dead yet.

I settled on black slacks and a cheerful sweater—a nice balance between here and there. I got in the car, and Jeff—who has a very Virgo sense of humor—was playing Mozart's *Requiem*.

I said it reminded me of the scene in *Amadeus* when a wagon was rumbling away with Mozart's shrouded body in a re-usable casket.

"And then they threw him in a common grave and covered him with lime," said Jeff. "And that was it."

In case you've ever wondered who is the straight man in our comedy team, he is.

Well, we got to Green Hill and my cell phone rang. It seemed that the top grave man who was supposed to meet us was unable to make it. Another cemetery worker was on his way to show us around.

We took a few minutes to drive around the cemetery, which is very old—it opened in 1877—and consequently full of old Greensboro families. The Weavers. The Lindleys. The Zenkes. Some of the stones are old and ornate. Some are very, *um*, different.

We commented on headstones as we passed, much as you might critique homes if you were hunting for a new place to live, which we were in a way, with the obvious exception of the "live" part.

"I like that," I said, pointing out one marker.

"Yeah, that's nice," Jeff said.

"Oh, my God!" I said.

"What?"

"Can you believe anyone would be buried under that?" I said.

"Maybe it was added later," Jeff said, giving the dearly departed the benefit of the doubt.

That's when Mark showed up in his city truck, and we followed him to one of the available areas, which was on a slope beside a creek. Mark corrected me and said it was a drainage ditch.

Okay, it was a drainage ditch. That occasionally fills with water. And runs. Like a creek.

"Does it ever flood?" I asked.

Mark hesitated.

"Let me put it another way," I said. "Has anyone ever popped up?"

"No," Mark said, clearly relieved that he could report good news. "Nobody's popped up."

He got out a big loose-leaf notebook and laid it on the tailgate of his truck. He flipped through it and jabbed a finger at a map of the available plots around the drainage ditch.

We surveyed the scene. True, these were partial waterfront lots— er, plots—and they offered peaceful views. But I was wary of the slope.

I imagined a graveside service where people struggled to maintain their balance. I imagined leaning headstones. I imagined my yet-to-be-born grandchildren coming to mourn me—because I was one hell of a grand-mother—and slapping at mosquitoes that bred in the drainage ditch.

"Let's goooooooo," the kids would whine.

Jeff's concern was entirely different. I knew that, with him being a civil engineer and having inherited his maternal grandmother's irrational fear of water under the house, he was never going to go for a grave in a low-lying area. I mean, if he thought water was under his vault, he would die. Again.

We asked what else was available in that area. Mark said not much. He said that occasionally people would buy a whole bunch of plots, thinking everyone in the family would want to be buried there, then things would change. Children would move off, get married, and have families, and decide they'd rather be buried somewhere else.

So then the family would try to sell off the extra spaces in the family plot, but that was problematic because often there was a big ol' family headstone spanning the spaces or maybe, back when it was allowed, the family had fenced off their plots with a wall or a granite curb.

"Who wants to be buried in someone else's pen?" Mark asked.

Good point. I never could totally rest in peace in another family's pen.

Mark said there was one other section in Green Hill with available spaces, so we followed him along the narrow, winding, root-buckled roads to an area near the corner of Battleground Avenue and Hill Street.

The graves were within view of a Mexican restaurant.

"I do not want to be buried next to a Mexican restaurant," Jeff said.

"Why not?" I said. "It would be fun, especially during Cinco de Mayo."

I nodded in the direction of NewBridge Bank Park, where the Greens-boro Grasshoppers play baseball a few blocks away. "And, look, we could see the fireworks after home games."

I admit that I briefly fantasized about our boys with their friends and families coming to our graves on Fourth of July nights, when the Hoppers blow it out with fireworks.

72

"Hey, let's go over to Mom and Dad's," they'd say. "They have a great view."

Never mind that the cemetery closes at sunset. The gatekeeper would be touched and let it slide until the *boom* and *ahhh.*

Jeff snapped me out of my daydream.

"It's too loud here," he said. "And look how close we'd be to the road."

Forty yards away, a road crew worked on Hill Street. They backed up a piece of equipment.

Beep-beep-beep-beep.

It was enough to wake the dead. Plus, I noticed barbed wire across the top of the cemetery fence. I thought of an old joke:

    Q: Why is there a fence around a cemetery?

    A: Because people are dying to get in.

But this was no joke. This was dead serious.

We asked Mark a few questions. What about the plantings? The green kind, that is. One thing we liked about Green Hill was that it's full of wonderful old trees and shrubs, and many of the trees have markers saying what they are.

Mark said "that Craft man" — meaning the late Bill Craft, Greensboro's Johnny Appleseed — had planted a lot of the greenery, and that people who were buried there could plant things beside their headstones as long as they got approval.

But — and this was a big but — he said that if we went that route, we should not plant boxwoods because they would attract bees, and the bees would sting city workers when they mowed, and the city workers would end up hating us.

Actually, if I liked boxwoods, that would seem like a chance worth taking. But I don't like boxwoods because they smell like cat pee, and I said so. Mark and I nodded a nod of mutual understanding.

I could tell that Mark knew a lot about the burial business, so I asked him if it was true that you couldn't be buried in a pine box in your yard because, honestly, I'm drawn to the simplicity of the idea.

Mark said that if you lived out in the county where there was no zoning, you could be buried in your yard. But if you lived inside the Greensboro city limits, no, you could not be buried in your backyard—and you wouldn't want to be buried in a pine box anyway because a pine box rots and then the ground above it sinks.

I started to ask whether a depression in your backyard wouldn't be a nice place for a koi pond later, but I let it go because I started thinking about the movie *Poltergeist*, in which a family moves into a haunted house where spirits come in through the TV. Later there's a hellacious storm, and the ground gets saturated, and skeletons start popping up all over the neighborhood. (See earlier question about popping up.)

And it occurred to me that that's what could happen if everyone started getting buried in a pine box in her backyard. Some slacker in the family would be put in charge of making the grave, and he'd dig down a foot or so and say, "There, that's good enough," and a few weeks later a gully washer would hit, and all of sudden you'd be springing up out of the ground like a Pop-Tart out of a toaster. It's not something that would increase your property value or your popularity with the homeowners' association.

We thanked Mark and made an appointment to see Forest Lawn.

Well, the day we went to Forest Lawn was beautiful. Sunny, warm, breezy. I know that shouldn't have figured into our impression of the place, but it did. I thought, "Wow, I could see myself not living here."

Not only that, I noticed headstones of several families that I knew and liked. There were the Schlossers. And the Kirkmans. And the Dodsons.

Over there were the Aydelettes who started Yum Yum, the high altar of hot dogs and ice cream across from UNCG. How cool would it be to be buried close to hot dog and ice cream people? I could practically feel a party coming on.

This time, we were riding around in a car with Mike, the head grave man whom we'd missed at Green Hill. Mike gave us the grand tour, pointing out the things that make Forest Lawn so attractive to potential grave-owners. One is the option of having upright headstones, which some private graveyards do not allow.

Mike explained how your upright markers allow for a little more creativity than your flat markers, though your uprights cost more, especially if you get into dark granites and detailed etchings. Also, upright markers are easier for the bereaved to find.

I know how important that is. There's nothing worse than traipsing around a graveyard, trying to find a flat marker. You feel like you've lost your car in a parking lot. "I'm sure we parked her over here. Didn't we?"

Another selling point of Forest Lawn, Mike said, was the trees. People love to be buried under trees. I asked why. Did they feel like they needed the shade? I mean, wasn't it kind of cool underground anyway? He smiled and shrugged. "I've been a funeral director for twenty-five years, and there's no rhyme or reason to funerals and burials," he said. "You have to have a sense of humor about it. If you don't have a sense of humor, you won't survive."

I thought that was pretty profound, coming from a grave man.

Mike continued his tour. Over there, he said, was a man who moved here from New York. He bought sixteen plots. He directed his heirs to bury him smack in the middle and leave the rest of them empty.

"He said he was tired of fighting crowds," Mike said.

He pointed out the final resting places of some of Forest Lawn's more prominent residents. There was a textile magnate Chuck Hayes, who was entombed first at Lake Lure and later in an above-ground crypt at Forest Lawn; as earthy as he was, Chuck did not want to be buried in the ground.

Over there, Mike said, was the mausoleum of the Sternberger-Benjamin family, whose Starmount Company developed Friendly Center and the Starmount Forest neighborhood. They first erected their classical little mausoleum—which sleeps eight—in the Hebrew Cemetery on High Point Road, but the family moved the whole shebang to Forest Lawn in the 1950s.

Over there, Mike said, was Sandy Bradshaw, the Greensboro flight attendant who died on September 11, 2001, when terrorists hijacked United Airlines Flight 93. Her plane went down in Shanksville, Pennsylvania.

Once, when I was doing a newspaper story on the anniversary of 9/11, Sandy's mother, Pat Waugh, took me to the grave and talked about her daughter. Sandy had lived with her husband and two young children just down the road from that still spot. Every time I walk my dogs on the loop around the Guilford Courthouse National Military Park, I look through the fence at the American flags and yellow roses that Sandy's family keeps on her grave, and I think about her. I wonder where her kids are now. I never knew them, but I think about them, and I wish them well. Wherever they are, I'm sure there are only a few degrees of separation between us. Living in one place for a long time will do that to you.

As we rode around with Mike, my mind skipped to my own boys and all the great times our family has had in the parks surrounding Forest Lawn. Pushing strollers, feeding ducks, riding bikes, picking up kids from Safety Town, smacking tennis balls at the J. Spencer Love Tennis Center (Spencer Love himself is in Forest Lawn), watching our dogs race around at the Bark Park, lying in the grass in front of the General Greene statue and listening to Music for a Sunday Evening in the Park.

It turned out that Jeff was thinking about those things too and how fitting it would be to leave whatever's left of us in the area where we'd already left so much of us.

We decided to buy plots at Forest Lawn. We hope we won't need them for a while, but when we do, drop by and see us. I can't tell you what the marker will look like yet, but I can tell you that Jeff is leaning toward the flat kind (bring your GPS), whereas I am lobbying for a stone in the style of a garden bench, the kind with your name carved into the back of the bench.

Jeff says no one will sit on a gravestone, but I think they might if we have seat cushions. And cupholders. Maybe a couple of Tiki torches. We're still ironing out the details.

In any case, we'll be on high ground. In the shade. With no boxwoods. BYO fireworks and margaritas.

MARIA JOHNSON graduated from the University of Kentucky in her hometown of Lexington. In a Disney-esque, circle-of-life turn, her first job brought her to Greensboro, where her mother had graduated from Woman's College, now UNCG. After working as a newspaper writer for a zillion years and winning several state and national awards, Maria became a freelancer. She's now a humor columnist and contributing editor at *O.Henry* magazine. She and her husband have two wonderful sons, one cunning beagle, and a big galoot of a foxhound.

Views from Before

Hamburger Square Has a Past

JIM SCHLOSSER

MY FIRST EXPERIENCE WITH HAMBURGER SQUARE came as a little boy visiting my grandfather, who managed a general store near the square. I saw nothing unseemly about the place. Just a bunch of old buildings, the smell of tobacco from a cigar factory, and men wearing dungarees and khaki work clothes who labored in a rail freight yard adjacent to the square.

It wasn't until after I became a newspaper reporter that I saw in person why many people avoided these four corners with an odd name. It was the late 1970s. I was starting my research for a story about a group of winos that frequented the square.

My starting point was Jim's Lunch, a drinking place with a perfect generic name. As I entered, I was nearly toppled by a man leaving in a hurry. Right behind him came another man also in a rush. He wielded a long knife that must have come from the kitchen. I was told later he was attempting to administer some street justice.

Today, nearly all who gave the square its nasty reputation are gone: the winos, the half-dozen seedy hotels, Jim's Lunch, and that other cheap beer and burger joint, the California Sandwich Shop (originally called the California Fruit and Wienie Stand), the last two mainly responsible for giving rise to the square's name in the 1920s. Missing too are the shabby State Theatre and once-elegant National Theatre, which in 1956—and still a decade away from being demolished—booked Elvis Presley for a one-day stand. This was just prior to Presley's appearance on *The Ed Sullivan Show*, which led to him becoming a national heartthrob.

Even at its worse, the square was a place of fascination.

Early in my lifetime and for a few decades before, it was the closest spot Greensboro had to a "red light district." One urban legend that arose at the end of World War II had Greensboro with the highest VD rate in the nation, and Hamburger Square allegedly the epicenter of the epidemic. That was back when Greensboro had a wartime Army Air Corps base within the city limits. Between its opening in 1943 and closing in 1946, the base processed 330,000 soldiers, including the future Hollywood star Charlton Heston, who got married here in 1944, a union that lasted until his death in 2008.

Soldiers were drawn to the square. They could buy cheap beer, greasy food, and if lucky find a woman. No statistics support the claim of the city being the nation's VD capital, but it makes for a good story for those who love writing and talking about Greensboro's downtown, particularly the south end that includes the square.

While the VD story may be a myth, it is true that the city leaders who lobbied vigorously for the Army Air Corps to build a base here lobbied as hard at the war's end to get rid of it.

But to remember Hamburger Square only for sleaze and seediness does it an injustice. Greensboro residents don't fully appreciate or even know that history was made in the square in the nineteenth century and famous men politicked there in the early twentieth century.

Though its history is obscured, its buildings are celebrated. Architecture left from earlier times draws visitors with cameras and paint canvasses. Benjamin Briggs, executive director of Preservation Greensboro, says no other big city in the state has as many venerable facades in its downtown. Many of those are on Hamburger Square and in the 200 and 300 blocks of South Elm Street that feed into the square.

The buildings feature Ionic pilasters, arched windows, and hand-carved medallions. Some façades retain what are called *ghost signs:* faded reminders of businesses long gone, such as the words *Sapp Sells It Cheaper* on a storefront at 318 South Elm where the Sapps operated a store eighty years ago.

South Elm and Hamburger Square retain so many old commercial buildings that the area has been designated a National Register of Historic Places District.

But even before those historic buildings were erected, two important events occurred in the square. One was vital to the city's present well-being—the coming of the railroad. The other was vital to keeping the United States one nation—the ending of the Civil War in the North's favor.

In 1856, a railroad construction gang working its way from the east and another working from the west linked in what would eventually become Hamburger Square. That link was momentous: There the last spike was driven in the North Carolina Railroad, creating the first east-west line across the state, from Goldsboro to Charlotte.

Trains immediately began rumbling across the South Elm Street crossing, carrying freight and passengers, and during wartime, troops and war supplies. As a result of the railroad, Greensboro and the rest of North Carolina ceased being "The Rip Van Winkle State."

A primitive depot went up beside the South Elm Street rail crossing in the square. People of all types brushed each other catching trains to distant places, such as Montana, and nearby places such as Rudd, a flag stop ten miles north of downtown next to what's now the city's Bryan Park recreational complex.

Between 1856 and the late 1880s, new rail lines radiated from Greensboro in six directions. The Confederate army in 1864 built a line that veered north from the N.C. Railroad line near Hamburger Square to Danville,

Virginia, where it connected to a line to Richmond and from there to Washington and New York. The railroad transformed Greensboro from a somnolent backwater village without any natural attraction into what's now the state's third largest city, with a 2014 population of 270,000.

Those rails led to Hamburger Square's second historic occasion. A train from Richmond brought Confederate President Jefferson Davis and his cabinet to the square in April 1865. They were fleeing the Yankees, who were closing in on the Confederacy capital. Greensboro likes to believe it was the last capital of the Confederacy, although Charlotte makes the same claim because Davis and his cabinet went there after leaving Greensboro. A more supportable claim can be made that the Civil War ended here. Davis and his honchos spent three days in Greensboro, holding meetings in a railcar parked on a siding beside what's now Natty Greene's restaurant and brewery.

It was here Davis learned that Robert E. Lee had surrendered at Appomattox and realized for certain that the South had lost the war. He ordered the surrender of the Confederacy's largest fighting force, the Army of Tennessee, to Union General William T. Sherman. Sherman rode to the Bennett farm in Durham, where he accepted the surrender brought to him by General Joseph Johnston, commander of the Army of Tennessee.

As a result, some 90,000 Union and Confederate troops descended on Greensboro, which had a population of about 1500. The Union soldiers issued pardons to 40,000 vanquished Confederates, who stacked their arms and headed home. Mary Watson Smith, who kept a diary at the time, wrote of walking through the downtown and seeing blue-coated federal troops outside every building: ". . . the whole world looked blue — in unison with our feelings that bitter morning," she wrote.

Before Davis's arrival, Greensboro had a role in the aftermath of the last major clash between Southern and Northern troops, the Battle of Bentonville — fought from March 19 to 21, 1865, in eastern North Carolina. There Sherman's forces defeated Confederates under General Johnston. Trains then carried about 1000 wounded Southerners from Bentonville to

Hamburger Square. They were unloaded and sent to makeshift hospitals set up throughout downtown.

Many Southern cities were slow to recover after the Civil War. Greensboro, however, started growing and prospering—because of the railroad. In 1870, the North Carolina General Assembly granted Greensboro a new charter officially elevating its status to that of a "city" instead of a "town."

By 1890, more than forty passenger trains were stopping at the two depots in the square. That year an editor of the *Greensboro Daily Record*, the city's first daily newspaper, coined "The Gate City" as Greensboro's nickname. Greensboro had become akin to what the Atlanta airport would be years later: You couldn't get anywhere without first going through it—in the case of Greensboro, through Hamburger Square.

During one year some 76,000 train tickets were sold in Greensboro.

In 1899, Southern Railway, which by then had leases on most rail lines out of Greensboro, built a station in Hamburger Square fit for a growing city. The red-brick building had turrets, gables, and other architectural touches that made it perhaps the city's grandest building at the time. Another small depot across the tracks served the Cape Fear and Yadkin Valley Railway from Wilmington to Mount Airy.

During political seasons, the square filled with people coming to see presidential candidates speak from the rear of rail cars. Three-time candidate William Jennings Bryan came several times to speak, and another to eat breakfast at the Huffine Hotel on the square while waiting to change trains. Bryan was aboard the train that in 1906 brought the body of Charles Duncan McIver to the square. McIver, the founder of State Normal and Industrial College (then renamed Woman's College and today known as UNCG), had died on the train while traveling with Bryan. McIver had been a frequent visitor to the square since he started the college in 1891. He made it a point to greet the trains bringing students to his all-women's college.

More than 10,000 people stood in the square to hear Teddy Roosevelt speak from the rear of a train in 1905. In 1935, the other Roosevelt, Franklin, spoke in the square from the rear of the presidential train car, the Ferdinand Magellan. Thousands came to Hamburger Square ten years later, on the night of April 13, 1945, when FDR's funeral train passed through on its way from Warm Springs, Georgia, to Washington.

Photos also show thousands in the square celebrating the city's centennial in 1908. The centennial gate stood tall in the square.

For all the good it brought to the city, the railroad caused chaos in Hamburger Square. Idling trains blocked pedestrians, horseless carriages, and horse-pulled ones from getting past the South Elm crossing. The past and the present met in the square. A mule pulling two women in a carriage panicked at the sight of a locomotive hissing and backing over the crossing. A police officer managed to calm the animal and prevented the carriage from overturning.

Greensboro's human population was more tolerant of the railroad. Behind nearly all positive economic events of the past the railroad lurks.

The Cone brothers would later cite Greensboro's rail connections as a reason they started their textile factory empire here in the 1890s, after first founding the Cone Export & Commission Company to market textile products for other manufacturers. The Cones moved their export office from New York to Greensboro in 1893 occupying a building a block from the square.

Three Cone factories arose in northeast Greensboro. They became the city's biggest employer for decades. Only one of their mills, the White Oak plant, still remains. But the Cone legacy still benefits Greensboro. Cone Health Care System, started with Cone money and now owning hospitals and medical services, ranks as the area's biggest employer.

Greensboro cigar makers opened for business in the early twentieth century, again because the railroad could easily bring in raw tobacco and ship out cigars. From the early 1900s to the 1950s, fourteen local companies produced stogies and another manufactured colorful cigar boxes. A 1922 news story reported that Greensboro made 300,000 cigars over a twenty-four-hour period. The best-known brands were El Moro and El-Rees-So, both made by the El Moro Cigar Company, which dates to 1915 and eventually built a large factory next to Hamburger Square.

El Moro employed three hundred people, boasting that all of its cigars "are made by girls—pretty girls." The company didn't mention it got by with paying women lower wages.

El Moro was the last of Greensboro's cigar makers in 1955 when it was bought by an outside company and moved to Pennsylvania. Until then the aroma of leaf was the square's signature. It wafted twenty-four hours a day. The state recently erected a highway historical marker in the square to celebrate the city's cigar industry that almost rivaled in size those in Tampa and Baltimore.

Spencer Love, who founded Burlington Mills (later Burlington Industries) in 1923 and made it the world's largest textile maker, credited Greensboro's rail connections for his decision to move his company's headquarters from Burlington to Greensboro.

Once again, the railroad was a selling point the city used to convince the state in the early 1890s to build two state colleges here—what are now North Carolina A&T State University and the University of North Carolina at Greensboro.

The railroad was also a factor in the army's decision to turn 600-plus acres off Summit Avenue into a base during World War II, because the railroads could easily move soldiers in and out of the city.

When the federal government started the federal highway system, the new highways tended to parallel railroads. With so many rail lines in so many directions, Greensboro wound up with four major highways—U.S. 29 North and South, U.S. 421 South and West, U.S. 70 East and West, U.S. 220 North and South—all merging at Elm and Market streets.

In the 1950s, when the Eisenhower administration started the interstate highway system, it followed the routes of the first generation of highways, which of course had followed the railroads. As a result, Greensboro emerged with two interstates, I-85 and I-40, passing through the southern side of the city. It was rare for a city of its size to have two super highways.

The vast number of travelers who changed trains in the square or who drove through the city often needed a place to sleep. Consequently, six hotels arose in the 1890s. The Clegg, which opened in 1891, was the most elegant. Located across from the depot, it had a large dining room, a bowling alley, a barbershop, and other conveniences. Once, an itinerant artist offered to paint a mural for the dining room. The hotel agreed, and gave him room and board in return. He painted an apple green Southern Railway steam locomotive pulling passenger cars through a rural setting. It became a local landmark.

Over the decades, however, the hotels deteriorated as new ones, such as the O. Henry and the thirteen-story King Cotton, opened north of the square. Most travelers no longer wanted to stay at the little hotels next to the railroad tracks. The square's hotels survived by catering to less fashionable travelers and working people who toiled in Greensboro and lived elsewhere. The hotels rented rooms long-term or for a few hours. In 1927, an unmarried couple checked into the Huffine and soon heard a knock on the door. The police hauled them away intending to charge them with occupying a room for immoral purposes. A deal was brokered. The cops said if the couple agreed to marry on the spot, right there in the police station, no charges would be filed. The desk sergeant, who happened to be an ordained minister, officiated at the wedding.

The Clegg Hotel, which had been run by a respectable family, started receiving some bad press. In the 1950s, the son of a prominent businessman who lived in the posh Irving Park neighborhood was nabbed there with a prostitute. The newspapers splashed the story big, causing people to comment, "Ah, that's Hamburger Square for you."

The Clegg was torn down in the 1970s, but fortunately its mural was rescued and now belongs to the Greensboro Historical Museum.

It was sometime in the 1920s that Hamburger Square began losing its luster as a business address. Years earlier in 1893, Simon Schiffman was waiting to change trains in Greensboro when he took a walk along South Elm. There, he spotted a bankrupt jewelry store for sale and bought it. While Schiffman's Jewelers went on to become a national chain, it eventually joined other retailers in moving out of the square and farther north to the new downtown retailing center.

Another blow came in 1927 when Southern Railway (now Norfolk Southern) built a new depot, the largest in North Carolina, two blocks east of the South Elm crossing. The old depot in the square still stands, but its turrets and gambles and platforms are gone.

Jim's Lunch on the ground floor of the Piedmont Hotel—which renamed itself the MacArthur near the end of World War II—came to symbolize a low-class drinking place in Greensboro. When business people at the sophisticated north end of downtown discussed where to eat lunch, you could count on one wise guy to generate derisive guffawing by suggesting Jim's Lunch.

Something about Jim's Lunch's created anger, like that displayed by the man with the knife chasing another man.

Jack Fuquay, the best known of the square's winos, once got mad at Jim's Lunch's owner after apparently being ejected from the premises. Jack responded with a crowbar that obliterated the eatery's big picture windows. Jack, a World War II vet who slept on the ground behind the square's Bob Hatters shoe-shine place (a rare black-owned business in the downtown), resembled "Soapy," the character in the story "The Cop and the Anthem," by Greensboro native O. Henry. As winter approached, Soapy repeatedly failed at trying to get arrested so he could enjoy the warmth of a jail cell. Same with Jack Fuquay. He had a bellyache and wanted medical attention guaranteed to those in jail. He shoplifted. No cops came running. He broke a store window. No one seemed to care. Frustrated, he approached a police officer and asked, "What does a guy have to do to get arrested, slug a cop?" He proceeded to do just that and got the free medical care he wanted.

The California Sandwich Shop, which was on the ground floor of the Harris Hotel, managed to lure a few coat-and-tie types to the square. Its hot dogs were that good. Never mind that the proprietor lined buns with wieners along his hairy arm while adding mustard, slaw, onions, and chili.

Evidence of the winos could be seen by the number of discarded bottles of Richards Wild Irish Rose, a cheap wine in a screw-cap bottle. Ironically, the brand traces its origins to a half block from Hamburger Square. Car-Cal Winery started here in 1936, importing grapes from California and fermenting them into wine. In the 1940s, Car-Cal moved to New York, where it became Canandaigua Winery and started making Richards Wild Irish Rose. It grew into one of nation's largest wine-makers.

When a wino passed out in Hamburger Square, it was usually on one of the benches. After merchants and others complained of sloshed men zonked out at midday, the city removed the benches.

Today, the square is gentrified. The renewal of the entire downtown, pretty much dead by the 1980s, began in Hamburger Square. An organization called the Old Greensborough Preservation Society pushed to save the old storefronts and to encourage new businesses to locate in them. To add Yule cheer, one new retailer painted large vegetable cans green and red and decorated a giant magnolia tree in a small park that forms the square's fourth corner.

In the mid-1980s, investors poured money into converting an old lingerie plant on both sides of South Davie and several commercial buildings on South Elm into apartments called Greensborough Court at Hamburger Square. When the ninety-nine apartments were nearly completed, they were destroyed by the worst fire in the downtown's history. The developers rebuilt them and today they are known as "The Lofts." Why Hamburger Square was dropped from the name in 2001 is not clear.

Those apartments and brave pioneers who bought old buildings during the 1970s in which to work and live introduced residential living to the downtown. This hastened revival and added a nice touch to South Elm, with residents walking their dogs.

A new condo project, Smothers Place, stands on the former site of the Clegg Hotel. A two-floor wing of what was the Clegg remains over the former Blumenthal's store. The store's ground floor has been subdivided into retail space. The old hotel wing above is now Blumenthal's Apartments. The apartments have been modernized, but the late Bob Blumenthal, son of the founder, kept a reminder of bygone days by using the hotel's doors, pine floors, and beams.

The square's best-known restaurant is Natty Greene's, occupying the old California Sandwich Shop, which lasted into the 1980s as did Jim's Lunch. Natty's has incorporated the upper two floors of what was the Harris Hotel into the restaurant. Natty's has become regionally renowned for its home-made beers.

Jim's Lunch is now a comedy club. The upper floors of what was the MacArthur Hotel are occupied by a restaurant and an upscale billiard parlor. M'Coul's Public House thrives at the site of the old El Moro cigar factory. Across the street, the old Carolina Hotel has been gutted and turned into condos.

The name Hamburger Square lives on through the *Hamburger Square Post,* a monthly newspaper that started in the 1970s when the square was at a low point in retail activity. *The Post* has held on long enough to cover the square's renaissance of new restaurants, apartments and condos, and retailers. Starting on Thursday nights, the sidewalks in and around the square fill up with people coming to Natty Greene's, Grey's Tavern, M'Coul's, and other new businesses in old buildings.

A traffic circle formerly in the square vanished when roundabouts went out of style with traffic planners. Now, they are back in fashion. The city built a new one about ten years ago a block from the square at McGee and South Greene streets. A statue of the city's namesake, General Nathanael Greene, decorates the circle. Never mind Greensboro already had a huge statue of Greene at Guilford Courthouse National Military Park.

An opportunity was missed to honor nineteenth-century Governor John Motley Morehead, whose Blandwood Mansion stands nearby. As governor in the 1840s and later as private citizen, Morehead was the foremost person in getting the railroad built that made Greensboro grow and brought about the founding of Durham, Burlington, High Point, and other cities along the N.C. Railroad line. He also persuaded the general assembly to build the east-west railroad. After leaving office, he politicked to make sure the route didn't follow a straight line from Goldsboro to Charlotte, which would have taken it south near Sanford.

Instead, the rails arched north passing through Morehead's hometown and what's now Hamburger Square.

One aspect of the square remains unchanged. Everyday, at all hours since 1856, trains have jolted the peace in Hamburger Square.

Anyone who dares complain knows nothing about Greensboro's history.

JIM SCHLOSSER is a Greensboro native, and spent most of his career as a general assignment reporter for the *Greensboro Record* and then the *News & Record*. He covered hurricanes, major sports events such as the Super Bowl and NCAA Final Four, national political conventions, presidential inaugurations, and Greensboro history. He retired in 2008, but wrote a weekly column for two years for the *News & Record*. He recently retired for a second time, as a contributing writer for *O.Henry* magazine.

A Nice Nasty Town

LINDA BEATRICE BROWN

We are going to have rioting. We are going to have people killed.
—Edward Zane, Greensboro City Council member, 1960

"As I walked to my classes under the walkway leading from one building to the next there was a rainfall of eggs coming from the classroom building. Most of them landed on me. But I wiped my face, looked in disgust at my new dress and walked on to class. Some of the students jeered and called out "nigger." Some students yelled, "You know we don't want you here. Go back to your own school. This is our school!"

There was a strange call from a man who identified himself as the Grand Wizard of the Klan. He said, "You are helping to destroy all that is sacred to the Southern way of life. If you go to Senior High you will live to regret it." All I could think of as I listened to him condemn me to hell was I wanted to smother him. This ongoing harassment was joined by others who identified themselves as members of the White Citizens' Council; they talked mostly about how "the good Lord did not intend for blacks to go to school with whites." My brothers told me later that members of the Klan and other groups threw things down our chimney. We were lucky that nothing exploded when it landed in the fireplace. White men would come by and cut up or puncture the tires to our car and truck. Many of our animals were killed and we mourned the death of our beloved dog. A tree was cut down across our driveway making it impossible for us to get out until my brothers cut it up into logs.

Our calls to the police were in vain. They did not provide any significant protection and said, "There is nothing we can do to prevent these disasters from happening." Students would regularly throw rocks at our car. I found tacks in my seats in the classroom. The incident that hurt the worst was the loss of my father's snack bar. It inexplicably burned down. That was the only time that I saw my father cry. He just said "Why this, why this?" I wanted to know what it was about being Black that made it necessary to have separate restrooms and water fountains for us in Woolworth and other downtown stores."

This is the voice of Josephine Boyd (Bradley) who was the first black student to attend Greensboro Senior High. She (and her parents) took the bold step of desegregating the city's oldest high school in 1957. Josephine was only seventeen and was alone in her action. Through her story we gain a sense of Greensboro's racially divided atmosphere a few years before the Bennett College and North Carolina A&T students walked out of their dorms to the Woolworth's lunch counter and into history. Today many people know about the Woolworth sit-ins in 1960. Before that, however, Josephine Boyd and others also defied the cultural norms of Greensboro.

It could be said that there were at least two cultures in Greensboro at that time, the *official* culture and the *real* culture. On the surface the commonly held image of the city, and indeed of North Carolina, was that this was an area more progressive than much of the South. Underlying that veneer was a different reality. Willa Player, who was then president of Bennett College, the historically black women's college, said Greensboro wanted to maintain its image of niceness while sustaining racial segregation: "I think it was erroneous to think of Greensboro as a liberal city. It did just enough to appear to the outside world to be less segregated than other cities."

Whites who challenged the traditional Southern way and the status quo were also met with hostility, as Ginger Parker and two other white students discovered when they made an effort to support Josephine Boyd at Greensboro High. Jennie Parker, Ginger's mother, remembers:

> Our daughter and a few friends went to Josephine and told her they would like to eat with her in the lunchroom. At least one day I went out and sat with them. Things were thrown, marbles, all sorts of things like that. Our daughter and one of the other students received threatening phone calls saying things like, "How does it feel to be a nigger lover?"

The men running the city and the business community didn't seem to understand that black frustration was hundreds of years old. The nature of the African American mindset was hidden in plain view, as it were, partly because of dissembling which black people had been practicing for so long, and partly because of the blindness of the white population. James Townsend, then city manager, later admitted that he had mistakenly believed that race relations in Greensboro had always been good. He, like many others, didn't understand that people denied equal access to the advantages of citizenship will at some point call for a reckoning.

Dr. George Simkins was a black dentist and civil rights activist during those years. Among his other battles, he led the fight to integrate Gillespie Golf Course in the Fifties. He recalled:

> Greensboro is a very, very conservative city. Greensboro is a very strange city in that blacks have to fight for everything that they get here. I mean they don't give one inch. And you have to picket, demonstrate, take them to court to get anything done. Other cities around

Greensboro—Durham, Raleigh, Winston-Salem, and High Point— were opening up their recreational facilities to people of color, whereas Greensboro was closing down everything. They would knock us down and we'd get back up and continue to fight.

Before and after Josephine Boyd walked into Greensboro High, there were many examples of the city's two cultures clashing in Jim-Crow–era Greensboro. The NAACP fought to desegregate public facilities—Moses Cone Memorial Hospital, public recreational facilities, and other public schools. All met with enormous resistance. Tensions flared. The same year Josephine Boyd entered all-white Greensboro High, a cross was burned on the Bennett campus, in front of the home of Professor Edward Edmonds, who had led an attempt to integrate the city's swimming pools.

When Woman's College professor Warren Ashby hosted groups of Bennett College and Woman's College students in his home, he received harassing phone calls. The violent shadow of racism was always skulking in the background, recalled Dr. Ashby in a 1981 interview:

> The white power structure and business community refused to acknowledge the real demands of the black community. It was pointed out to me by black members [of a faculty fellowship group] that they viewed Greensboro as a "nice nasty" town and when they would say "nasty," any white person would know that it was a lot nastier than it was nice for them.

Official Greensboro met *real* Greensboro on February 1, 1960, when four African American students from A&T sat down at the whites-only lunch counter at Woolworth's. The appearance of deference to whites had now been publicly broken.

By the second day of the sit-ins, student protesters endured heckling from the crowd. Groups of tough white teenagers flooded the store, while others drove by, yelling.

Once the sit-ins had started, three white students from Woman's College briefly joined the demonstration. Ann Dearsley, one of those students, gave a particularly detailed description of the intimidation she faced:

> There was a large white crowd behind us . . . Our position suddenly became clear, and the crowd became extremely threatening . . . It was a very scary three hours sitting in that lunch space because the crowd got closer and closer. There was a man with a knife behind my back. . . . It was obvious to me that the police would not support us and we sat there feeling really scared and totally unable to move because there were hundreds of people in that very narrow store. We said to each other how do we get out of here at 5:00? There were hundreds of hostile people filling the store and blocking the exits. . . . The store was full of angry people who didn't like what we were doing.

Saturday, February 6, was a nerve-racking day. A girl got her teeth knocked out by a thrown rock and other people were injured. Joseph McNeil, one of the original "Greensboro Four" who sat in at the Woolworth's counter, recalled a stink bomb being thrown at the picketers.

Longtime activist and sit-in participant Lewis Brandon remembered the tactic of harassment that was used against two men from A&T. His roommate, Donald Lyons, was burned by lighted cigarettes that attackers stuffed in his pockets. He recalled:

> Saturday morning, February 6, the Woolworth manager closed the counters. Things were very tense that day. Some white bullies began to move out of the way. The A&T football team had come downtown and at that time we had some guys weighing as much as 300 pounds. We went up to Woolworth and there was jostling for position at the counter. When they announced the counters were closed, we marched back to campus. As we walked past the King Cotton Hotel people threw bags of water and other things out the windows.

"We had nightly threats," said Jibreel Khazan, also one of the Greensboro Four. "People called and threatened to kill us. They said, 'We will kill you if you niggers go down there.'"

By the end of the first sit-in week, William Jackson from the Greensboro police said, "It looked like it was going to be very explosive."

Many white Greensboro citizens, according to newspaper accounts, reacted to the sit-ins with surprise and outrage, depending on their orientation. City leaders appeared to have been terrified at the prospect that a disruption of the status quo would cause chaos and bloodshed in the same city that was supposed to be so liberal. To put it another way, the story they wanted to tell about themselves was that their city was a "nice" city that maintained white supremacy.

Jo Spivey, a journalist with the *Greensboro Record,* reported that she was harassed by the Ku Klux Klan for covering this and other race-related stories. She explained that they called her house and frightened her young child, "scared her to death," she said.

As she covered the events that were unfolding, Spivey described the reactions of whites who were hostile to the protesting students:

> The spectators were more militant than the marchers. Sometimes they were hecklers; sometimes they were passive observers . . . some of them brought their kids to see it, which I couldn't understand. I saw some violence in the store, mostly pushing, jostling by some of the counter demonstrators.
>
> They didn't physically hurt these people but there were some white men, probably KKK members, who heckled the Bennett girls studying at the counter saying such things as, "Look at that nigger, she thinks she can read."

"We were determined we wouldn't get Greensboro into the headlines by having a riot where somebody was injured," said City Manager Townsend. George Roach, Greensboro mayor at that time, declined several requests for television interviews. "I was concerned about the national image of Greensboro. I wanted it to remain a local incident."

In the meantime, Edward Zane of the city council was telling the mayor and the council that something should be done about the sit-ins. He later admitted the council wanted segregation to remain. But he admonished them: "It will not work itself out. We are going to have rioting. We're going to have people killed. We're going to have a lot of bad publicity for the city of Greensboro."

Once the sit-in movement began, the black community experienced the entire range of Greensboro's race relations—from civilized and dignified exclusion to violence barely averted. The veneer was torn away, and the city could no longer claim that good relationships between blacks and whites ruled the day.

For example, no one could pretend any longer that it was accidental that the civilized community meetings of the YWCA, when blacks were invited, just happened *not* to be at a mealtime. No one could deny the taboo of blacks and whites eating together, a taboo that symbolized blacks' second-class citizenship.

Why did all this happen in Greensboro, and why in 1960? Although slavery ended with the Civil War, Jim Crow laws had been in place for generations. Josephine Boyd's efforts to end segregation in the Greensboro public schools followed the Supreme Court's decision to end segregation in all American schools in 1954. Martin Luther King led the famous Montgomery Bus Boycott beginning in 1955. By the Sixties, the country was ripe for change. Almost a century after the end of the slavery, young people from Greensboro, Bennett, and A&T knew something drastic had to be done if things were ever going to change.

Although the sit-ins began at the beginning of February, the lunch counter struggle continued for months. On March 31, students from Bennett and A&T picketed outside Woolworth's and other variety stores.

On April 5, Woolworth's and Kress closed. On April 22, forty-five A&T and Bennett students were arrested. The struggle continued.

Then on July 26, nearly six months after the first sit-in, the lunch counters in Greensboro's popular variety stores were opened to all.

There was much more work to do, but the sit-ins in Greensboro inspired a national response as the technique of nonviolent passive resistance spread from city to city. The humiliating and unjust practice of refusing people admittance and service based on their race ended in 1964 when President Lyndon Johnson signed the Civil Rights Act.

The young women and men who sat in at the Greensboro lunch counters were groundbreakers. Their courage helped to create a more just and equitable America for us all.

LINDA BEATRICE BROWN is the author of *Belles of Liberty, Gender, Bennett College and the Civil Rights Movement in Greensboro, North Carolina*. This view is adapted from that book. She is also the author of three novels and two books of poetry. She was Distinguished Professor of the Humanities at Bennett College until her retirement in 2013.

Safely Home

JIM DODSON

FUNNY WHAT YOU DON'T FORGET. I recall February 2, 1960, being a cold gray day in Greensboro, probably because it was my seventh birthday and I desperately hoped it might snow.

I'd only seen a dusting of snow once before in my young life, after all, during the year my family lived in a small town in South Carolina after my father lost his weekly newspaper in Mississippi. Ever since that dusting I'd been obsessed with seeing more real snow.

Greensboro was where my father's people — farmers mostly — had lived for at least six generations. Tate Street was named for my great-great-grandfather, George Washington Tate, an itinerate Methodist preacher and land surveyor who set out the modern boundaries of several Piedmont counties after the Civil War. My grandfather, whose name I bear, was a rural polymath named Walter who helped wire the Jefferson Standard building in the 1920s.

But all of this family history was still new to me that strange and fateful winter of 1960 following a long road home across a deep south beginning to stir with change. I was simply dreaming about seeing real snow for my seventh birthday.

We'd been back home in Greensboro less than a month, long enough for me to still be the quiet newcomer in Mrs. Chamberlain's second-grade class at Braxton Craven Elementary School near the Lindley Park apartments where we were staying while my folks hunted for a new house.

I'd asked for a new bicycle that had failed to come that Christmas. I was still trying to process the sweep of unexplained events that carried our family abruptly away from Gulfport, Mississippi, one November night in 1957, briefly to Wilmington and then to a pretty town called Florence, drowsing in the pines of South Carolina and the values of a vanishing age. In Florence, my dad worked for a long and difficult year at the newspaper.

On the face of things, my older brother, Dickie, and I knew little about these difficulties, though we understood that something had abruptly changed after our father drove to Memphis to purchase a new web press so that his fledgling weekly paper in Gulfport could expand to five days a week. He returned to Gulfport to discover that his "silent" partner in the operation, a linen-suited Burl Ives type who owned several shrimp boats and hoped to some day be governor of Mississippi, had cleaned out the newspaper's bank accounts and vanished for parts unknown with the shapely cigarette girl from a local hotel. That same day, my mother, seven months pregnant, suffered a miscarriage. Two days after this, word came that my dad's only sister, my Aunt Irene, had been killed in a car wreck on an icy road near Washington, D.C.

"That's the worst week I've ever heard of anyone having," I told him three decades later on the rainy night he finally told me about these difficult family events over warm beer in a drafty hotel on England's Lancashire coast, not far from where he'd been stationed just before D-Day. We were on a final trip together to play the golf courses where he'd learned to play the game during World War II.

"How on earth did you survive?"

True to his remarkably upbeat nature, though he was dying of cancer, he just smiled and sipped his beer. My nickname for my old man, bestowed when I was a know-it-all teenager, was Opti the Mystic.

"It's pretty simple, actually," he replied. "I had a wife I was worried about and two small boys to think about. Life is full of trials. Luckily I quickly found a job in Wilmington. That was a lifesaver that let us regroup. All I could think about, however, was eventually getting us all safely home to Greensboro."

Looking back, I enjoyed our mysteriously brief road stop in Florence even more than our two years in Wilmington. Florence is where I started school and had perfect attendance and learned to ride a bike and *feet-dance* to gospel music from the black maid who nursed our ailing mama back to health. But it was also a place where even I quickly grasped that a rigid racial order was strictly observed through the casual racism I heard and saw every day but couldn't quite name. It bumped hard against the values of both my parents, especially my mother.

She was a former West Virginia beauty queen raised by a stern German grandmother who had no tolerance for prejudice of any kind. Once, after I used a word that I heard commonly used by other grown-ups around me in Florence, my mother perp-walked me by the ear out of a crowded room and quietly warned me that if she ever heard the word *nigra* come out of my cute little mouth—the way *supposedly* educated white people say the n-word that was so taboo in our house—I would quickly find myself seated on the toilet thinking about my unfortunate choice of words with a brand-new bar of Ivory Soap clenched in my teeth.

The woman meant business. I never said that word again.

Ironically, not long after our maid passed away and we were the only white people who attended her funeral, that magical dusting of snow came to Florence. My brother and I went over to the country club to watch kids sled down a fairway. Two cops showed up and ran off a couple black kids who were about our age, actually knocking one of them to the ground. When I told my father about this, he merely shook his head.

Days later, out of the blue, we moved home to Greensboro. I'd never seen my mother and father so happy.

Which brings me back to Mrs. Chamberlain's class that gray, cold day in February, my seventh birthday.

We were drawing pictures of our favorite things when my father suddenly showed up at the classroom door a little before noon, asking that I be released from class.

Something was clearly up because brother Dickie was waiting in the hall with him, silent and blank-faced.

I guessed something was wrong with our mother.

And yet, as we walked out to Dad's new Pontiac Tempest he seemed perfectly fine, his old upbeat self.

"Is Mom okay?" I asked.

"She's fine, boys. I just thought we'd take our library books back and get new ones."

My brother and I exchanged glances.

This was clearly a ruse, code for something else in the wind. We'd had our library books only since Sunday afternoon. It was just Tuesday. Not even I, who was already reading on a fourth-grade level, read chapter books that fast.

We said nothing until we turned the corner from McGee onto South Elm and started toward the center of downtown. That's when we saw the crowds.

A large number of black people were gathered around the entrance of the Woolworth's Department Store. In my tender memory they were sitting and singing a gospel hymn of their own—though perhaps I'm confusing this with the next few days when the turn-out of folks supporting the nation's first peaceful sit-in demonstration grew several times larger and included students from A&T State, Bennett College, and Woman's College.

On this second day after the four brave A&T students quietly took seats at the Woolworth's counter and refused to leave when asked, the crowds were large but nothing like the seismic shock that soon spread across my native South within days and weeks—and soon swept across America itself.

We'd recently taken my mother to lunch after church at the fancy S&W Cafeteria on Market Street and walked around the corner to stand beneath the lighted marquee of the Center Theater, diagonally across the street from the crowds at the Woolworth's. There were plenty of policemen around and groups of white men who looked none-too-pleased.

I remember a great deal of heckling and nasty things being said, and one raw-boned, old man in particular who nudged me and pointed to a sign being held by a protester across the street that read *NAACP*.

"You know what that means, don't you, boy? It means *nigras ain't actin' like colored people.*" And then he chuckled. It was the same joke my father's boss in Florence liked to tell—the one that nearly landed me with Ivory soap in my mouth.

Dad moved us along the street.

"I wanted you boys to see this," he said. "This is history. You can tell your children about it. Everything is going to change after this—including that."

He was pointing to a small door beside the entrance to the theater. In my memory it was the "colored" entrance to the theater. Or maybe he simply told us what it was and what it symbolized in the Jim Crow South.

"That will be gone too," he said.

Mind you, my old man was no racial firebrand ready to walk across the street and join the historic protest. My mother would have been far more likely to do that. He was just a proud son of the South and the product of his time and place, a civilized but pragmatic Southerner who came from a rural family where character counted far more than race in the larger scheme of things. Going back to the Civil War, our ancestors had served in the Southern cause but were curiously opposed to slavery, something that took me years to reconcile. And during the bleak years of the Great Depression my grandfather allowed anyone passing his place and down on their luck, regardless of skin color, to stay in the room at the rear of his barn and even get a good meal. A black man named Willie stayed there and helped out on the farm for more than three years. Somewhere I still have a photo of the two of them posing by the barn in their dusty denim overalls, *Walter and William,* someone scrawled in a spidery hand on the back of the fading photo, 1934.

In a deeper context, I think my father's war experiences and professional travels across an awakening South, especially his time in racially charged Mississippi—not to mention my mother's feisty Germanic intolerance of intolerance—shaped his views.

Or maybe he simply understood the weight of history was turning over everything the old order valued in terms of social justice and human relations, even as we made our way home safely to Greensboro.

Whatever it was, not surprisingly, I followed his footsteps into journalism and went off to work on the largest magazine in the South, covering everything from bullet-headed Klansmen in Alabama to Jimmy Carter's presidency. Among other things I coached an all-black, inner-city baseball team to the league championship and fumed at the injustice when the coach of the all-white Buckhead champions proposed a metro Atlanta championship only to cancel it at the last minute, claiming his parents were "worried about trouble" if I brought my team out to their fancy ball field.

On a brighter note, I got to know Daddy King and traveled with Andy Young when he crossed Georgia running for governor, coming within a hair of winning and nudging history forward. Young was the first person to tell me, "In the South it's not how close the black man gets that bothers some white people, it's how big. In the North, it's the other way around."

He was right about this.

During the two decades I lived and worked in New England, I was frequently asked about growing up in the South—and Greensboro in particular—by folks who only knew the violent stereotypes, the clichés of racial intolerance that still haunt our landscape. They pointed to the infamous Klan shooting of 1979 as evidence of racial hatred simmering just below the surface of my hometown. I was always quick to come back with the historic sit-in demonstration of 1960 and point out that my high school—then the largest in the state—began busing in 1972, as did other high schools in the county, with only minor issues.

And yet I'm invariably transported back to the many powerful things I witnessed and heard during the first ten years of my life, part of a generation of fortunate white Southerners who came of age in a changed world that still has many miles to go, it would seem, before we can all claim to be safely home.

For what it's worth, I got a new Schwinn bicycle from Higgins Cycle Shop and a new sled from Sears for my seventh birthday.

I grew up riding that blessed bike all over Greensboro, attended a junior high on the south side that was racially mixed years before desegregation, played on several integrated ball teams, and flat wore out that old sled during the many snowy winters that came before I left home for college.

The allure of snow, I think, and a volume of Robert Frost poetry given to me by my favorite English teacher at Grimsley High were just two of the reasons I eventually took myself off to live in Maine.

Another important reason, I realize now, was that I needed to put time and space between the complex events of my Southern childhood and an adult life that belonged to a very different world.

My two happy decades on a snowy hilltop there made coming home a decade ago to North Carolina all the sweeter. My grown Yankee children love to come visit Greensboro, where their family roots run deep and they claim to feel right at home.

I hope that's true. I've never stopped feeling at home in Greensboro.

It was such a long and enlightening journey just to get here.

JIM DODSON is the founding editor of *O.Henry* magazine and the author of several best-selling books, including *Final Rounds* and *American Triumvirate*. He was recently awarded the Order of the Longleaf Pine for his writing. He is currently writing a book about the Great Wagon Road—the colonial road that brought the Irish, Scots, English, and Germans (including his ancestors) to the South in the early eighteenth century.

A Family Remedy

ASHLEY KAUFMAN

THE LITTLE BLUE JAR HAS BEEN SYNONYMOUS with cold relief around the world for nearly a hundred years. People most often apply Vicks VapoRub on the chest to ease their symptoms, but the Greensboro-born product inspires many uses not listed on the label. In a twist on tradition, some VapoRub loyalists rub the salve on their feet before bed to silence coughs, and use it to repel insects, cure nail fungus, and ease headaches—depending on whom you ask. My great-great-grandfather Lunsford Richardson would surely delight in his product's relevance today, more than a century after he mixed up the first batches in his Elm Street pharmacy. He dreamed of his medicine's rising to worldwide popularity, even when this prospect seemed as likely as azaleas blooming in the dead of winter.

Lunsford grew up on a large plantation along the Little River in Eastern North Carolina, but the Civil War claimed the family fortune that had been built over generations. He later recalled how the devastation of war shaped his hopes for the future:

> But, when a boy, I had determined to stick to my old state, thru thick
> and think [sic], and to assist with all the energy of my mind and body in
> helping her back to prosperity.

After graduating from Davidson College as salutatorian of his class, Lunsford spent four years teaching at the Little River Academy. He left the school to pursue a career in business, purchasing a pharmacy in the village of Selma near his childhood home. Happy to revisit his college interests in chemistry and Latin, he built a thriving concern, despite economic gloom that lingered after the war.

Eager to make his fortune in a larger town, Lunsford sold his drugstore and moved to Greensboro with wife, Mary Lynn, and their three children in 1891. Mary Lynn had grown up there, the daughter of First Presbyterian Church pastor Jacob Henry Smith and his wife, Mary. With sixteen manufacturing companies operating locally by 1891, Lunsford hoped to capitalize on the growing economy in his wife's hometown. Entrepreneurs from Northern states—including future textile tycoons and benefactors Moses and Cesar Cone—found appeal in Greensboro's location on the North Carolina Railroad. Sixty trains chugged through town every day, prompting the *Greensboro Daily Record* newspaper to christen Greensboro "the Gate City" in 1890.

After scouting out local pharmacies, Lunsford and business partner, John Fariss, purchased the Porter Drug Store at 121 South Elm Street from the uncle of William Sidney Porter (pen name O. Henry). Set in the bustling downtown district, the Porter store served as a popular spot to socialize, as well as shop. Men in business attire relaxed in front of the store on pleasant days and stayed warm by the fire in winter. Naming their store *Richardson-Fariss,* the new proprietors joined Elm Street merchants, including J.W. Scott grocery store, Odell Hardware, and J.M. Hendrix Company dry goods. To manage his new venture, Lunsford often worked long days—drugstores stayed open late to help customers in need of medicine at night.

The Richardson children relished occasional visits to the soda fountain at their father's store, where they ordered milkshakes to sip at little round tables.

The Richardson family built a home near downtown on land they received as a gift from Mary Lynn's parents. Lunsford and Mary Lynn celebrated the birth of son Lunsford Jr. soon after arriving in Greensboro, the baby joining older siblings Smith, Laurinda, and Mary Norris. (Daughter Janet Lynn would arrive in 1895.) From their new residence behind the Smiths' orchard and garden, the Richardson children could run to their grandparents' back porch in just a few minutes. As the grandchildren of a Presbyterian minister, the siblings were not allowed to play cards or dance. Fortunately, Presbyterians did not oppose sweets. Every Saturday night, Lunsford brought home a bag of candy for his children from West's Candy Kitchen downtown.

Lunsford soon presided over the most popular drugstore in Greensboro—establishing a new billing system to increase their cash flow. But Lunsford mostly found his passion in developing home remedies, creating his own formulas to help customers relieve headaches, coughs, and other common ailments. He experimented with a new remedy to ease his children's croup symptoms in 1894, blending an ointment of menthol, eucalyptus, and other natural ingredients. After proving its potency at home, Lunsford sold the product in his store as Richardson's Croup and Pneumonia Salve (renamed VapoRub in 1912). The croup salve expanded Richardson's line of home remedies, which included Little Laxative Pills and Yellow Pine Tar Cough Syrup. Finding his own name too long for a medicine label, he christened his line Vick Family Remedies, borrowing the name from his brother-in-law, Dr. Joshua Vick.

Despite earning raves around Greensboro, VapoRub was no overnight success. More than twenty years passed from the time Lunsford sold the first jars in his pharmacy to the salve's appearance on drugstore shelves across the country. Despite his talent for developing medicines, he did not possess natural marketing skills. After launching his own drug company, Vick Family Remedies, in 1905, Lunsford struggled to convince merchants outside the Greensboro area to carry his products. Even with limited funds to sustain the business, he believed his medicines would find their way into homes around the world.

It was a family enterprise from the start. Eldest daughter Laurinda joined the small staff at Vick Family Remedies as a secretary, applying the shorthand and stenography skills she learned at Greensboro Female College. She later reflected on the early days of her father's downtown production facility:

> He [Lunsford] rented two long adjoining rooms on Davie Street. In one [room] was a noisy bottling plant and the other was his office and manufacturing plant all combined. He sat on a high stool at a high desk with all his books and orders, etc., while a boy at the back behind the stove hammered the packing boxes and two women stirred the Vicks salve that Dad had mixed and they poured it into the little blue jars.

As he searched for a spark to boost Vick Family Remedies' profits, Lunsford also operated the first Pepsi distribution company in Greensboro to help support his family. Even so, his savings were nearly depleted. Lunsford hoped eldest son, Smith, could help jumpstart Vick's sales. Smith and younger brother, Lunsford Jr., had worked for their father growing up, helping to deliver prescriptions and make sales calls. After dropping out of Davidson College and being expelled from the United States Naval Academy, Smith went to New York to find a job and avoid his family's disdain. His tenacity and charisma made him a natural salesman. He worked in department stores before landing a job as a pitchman for the Beacon Blanket Company. But in 1906, he answered his father's call to return home to Greensboro, bringing back an abundance of confidence he had developed from his time in the big city.

Smith proposed dramatic changes after joining Vick Family Remedies, challenging Lunsford to retire his other medicines and sell only the croup salve. With strong competition for Vick's other remedies, Smith believed this unique salve presented an opportunity to stand out on store shelves. He also convinced his father to change the company name to Vick Chemical Company, reflecting its new focus on one product. The Vick's sales team set out first for the Blue Ridge Mountain region, where it won over steely merchants, one at a time. With no budget for advertising, Smith offered free sample jars with purchase of a VapoRub case to help introduce the product to customers.

Within a few years, Smith orchestrated VapoRub's roll out in general stores across the South. To accommodate the surge in orders, Lunsford constructed a new two-story headquarters on Milton Street in 1910. According to family members, he also purchased one of the first automobiles driven in town—an open model Hupmobile car to drive to and from the new factory outside downtown. Lunsford offered his children use of the car if they learned to drive, and Laurinda accepted the challenge. She wrote about navigating the car on roads usually traversed by horses: "All the roads were rough and dusty and full of mud holes and by the time we girls came home from a ride, our long hair and side combs and hairpins were all jolted loose." The Vick's sales team soon exchanged their horses for Ford Model T's, equipping the cars with ladders to hang VapoRub signs on trees and barns.

With his sons taking on more work at Vick Chemical (Lunsford Jr. joined the company in 1913), Lunsford Sr. could spend more time with his church and in the community. An elder of the First Presbyterian Church for twenty-seven years, Lunsford did not separate his faith from his business career, writing,

> I have done my work in the spirit of prayer, with God as my Senior partner, and giving my time, ability and money to building up his Kingdom in home and foreign fields.

Counting the children of slaves as his closest friends growing up, Lunsford felt passionate about supporting the black community in his adopted hometown. He paid for a nurse to provide medical care to black citizens and taught Sunday school in an impoverished Greensboro neighborhood known as "the bull pen."

The father-son partnership continued its success at Vick Chemical, as Smith and the sales team introduced VapoRub up north, then headed west. The country celebrated the end of World War I in November 1918, but another crisis threatened Greensboro and the nation. Spanish influenza struck its first North Carolina victims during the spring of 1918, rising to the level of an epidemic by the fall. With flu patients around the country suffering from respiratory symptoms, VapoRub sales soared into the millions within a year. Even adding extra shifts to the manufacturing plant in Greensboro, the company couldn't meet the demand from stores across the country. Vick ran newspaper advertisements with doctor-approved advice for flu treatment, one ad instructing patients to *Go to Bed and Stay Quiet—Take a Laxative—Eat Plenty of Nourishing Food—Keep Up Your Strength—Nature is the Only "Cure."*

The epidemic established Vicks as a national brand, but influenza brought tragedy along with fortune to the Richardson family. On a sales trip with son Smith across the West in 1919, Lunsford reveled in the popularity of his product in Colorado, Utah, and California, although he wrote to Mary Lynn that he felt homesick. In June, Lunsford fell ill in San Francisco. Smith detailed the increasing severity of his father's illness in telegrams home to Greensboro, writing to sister Mary Norris, "I can't take responsibility of withholding facts Dad is critically ill . . . please request prayers." Mary Lynn crossed the country by train to be by her husband's bedside, while the congregation at the First Presbyterian Church back in Greensboro prayed for his recovery.

However, he never recovered. On August 22, local newspapers lamented the death of Vicks founder, a *Daily Record* editorial proclaiming,

Mr. Richardson during the major portion of his life worked zealously for moderate financial reward and he witnessed the rich fruition of his undertaking only in recent years. When his greatest business successes came, however, they enabled him the more easily to promote his Greensboro interests, and he has been counted upon for liberality in all community undertakings for social and industrial betterment.

After a crowded memorial service at First Presbyterian, Lunsford was laid to rest in Green Hill Cemetery, a short walk from the home where his family had lived for nearly thirty years.

With demand continuing from the flu epidemic in 1919, annual Vapo-Rub sales soared from 11 million to 17 million jars. Lunsford's will divided Vick Chemical's stock between Mary Lynn and their five children, securing the family's control for the next generation. When the company went public in 1926—the *New York Times* declared, "The ambition of Lunsford Richardson . . . was realized yesterday, as was the ambition of his two sons who helped him to build the business, when his company, the Vick Chemical Company, was listed on the New York Stock Exchange." Just a few years after their father's death, Smith and Lunsford Jr. embraced his dream of creating a worldwide company by initially expanding into England and Mexico. After Vick's corporate headquarters moved to New York City in the late 1920s, the scent of VapoRub continued to waft from their factories in Greensboro. By 1929, Vick shipped its little blue jars to sixty countries around the world.

Ninety years after VapoRub's invention, Unilever waged a hostile take-over attempt on Vicks (renamed Richardson-Vicks in 1981). Because the Richardson family maintained about a one-third ownership stake in the company, it scrambled to boost its share to over 50 percent to gain more control. During the battle for Richardson-Vicks, the *News & Record* wrote about the Richardson clan's unity in the midst of turmoil: "Although the family itself now often is described as the Connecticut branch and the North Carolina branch, it has remained harmonious, as Unilever is finding out." Despite its solidarity and love of Vicks, the Richardson family could not overcome the dynamics of Wall Street. The board approved the friendly sale to Procter & Gamble in October 1985, securing a more favorable stock price and outcome for employees.

Former Richardson-Vicks chairman Smith Richardson Jr., son of Smith and grandson of Lunsford Sr., visited the Greensboro factories soon after the sale to discuss its impact with workers. Richardson relatives mourned the loss of their beloved company—impetus for closeness within the family tree for generations. Though Richardson kin would benefit financially from the sale, Eric Calhoun, great-grandson of Lunsford Richardson and Greensboro resident, said this windfall did not assuage their grief, "the family's first interest was in maintaining the company and it's a shame that hasn't happened. It's very definitely an occasion for mixed emotions." The family would still operate real estate and financial companies in Greensboro, as well as philanthropic funds and the leadership development nonprofit, the Center for Creative Leadership.

Though the Vicks sale devastated the Richardson family, their connection to VapoRub remained relevant to the brand's next chapter. Procter & Gamble named Vicks to its prestigious list of billion-dollar brands in 2012, recalling, *How a Simple Case of Croup Led to a "Truly Unique Product"* in Greensboro. When launching the new Vicks Nature Fusion line in 2011, P&G ran a television commercial featuring a portrait of Lunsford Richardson and a close-up of *Greensboro, North Carolina, U.S.A.* printed on a vintage VapoRub label.

Even though Vicks leaders had long feared a common cold cure could destroy demand for the product, Vicks VapoRub is still found in medicine cabinets around the world.

ASHLEY KAUFMAN works as a writer and communications consultant. Her writing has appeared in the *News & Record* and *Charlotte Magazine*. She is writing a book, titled *The Little Blue Jar*, about her family and their former company Vicks.

If These Walls Could Talk

Gone to Seed and Back Again at 400 Gorrell

LORRAINE AHEARN

THIS IS JUST A HOUSE, a prospective buyer might think, while crossing the creaky porch to the padlocked front door at 400 Gorrell Street.

It's just a house on a typical Southern street, the type that a hundred years ago would have been a posh address for the movers and shakers in town. They were engineers, bankers, doctors—people who could afford tile fireplaces and third-story turrets with commanding views.

They were people who later moved to Sunset Hills or Irving Park, leaving a perfumed garden to muddy ruin and screw-top wine bottles on a street where nobody wanted to walk after dark, and plenty avoided in daylight.

But nothing this drastic ever happens overnight. Not the revival of this house and its down-at-the-heels neighbors under the optimistically hip, new-urban name "SouthSide." And not the long, slow slide that brought these once-genteel houses down to shabby disrepair.

It's always a gradual thing. Like a thread pulled loose in a sweater, it goes unnoticed until it unravels so far that you can't mend it, you can't patch it, you can't hide it from polite company. Still, you wonder, stepping gingerly through the threshold here on the jagged edge of downtown. How did it get from there to here?

A century ago, at the crest of the Gilded Age when Greensboro first became a factory town, the house with the high ceilings and the wrap-around porch belonged to a white engineer. Gorrell was a "streetcar suburb"—among Greensboro's first—and the City Directory, yesterday's phone book, was organized in two sections—"White Department" and "Colored Department."

The lines held fast through World War II, after which black expectations began to rise, and prominent whites began moving away from the close-in neighborhoods such as Ole Asheboro and Arlington Park to new suburbs such as Sedgefield and Hamilton Lakes.

At 400 Gorrell, the engineer's widow stayed on into the 1940s, and then a black chef from the country club bought the house. It was a piece of a long-deferred dream, at least from his side of the table. After the chef died, his groundskeeper lived there. Then, like many of the once-opulent, too-big homes along Gorrell and Martin Luther King Jr. Drive, it was divvied up as apartments and rented to tenants who paid by the week.

Finally, the old Queen Anne fell to vagrants and addicts who used it as a flophouse. They carted off whatever fixtures and copper pipes they could pry loose and sell for scrap, until the city nailed the place shut and put up a *No Trespassing* sign. After that, the keys to 400 Gorrell belonged to no one, while urban planners waited for a developer to redo the blighted old neighborhood between downtown and Bennett College.

On a buzzing morning before the hot part of June, there is a whisper of camellias from the overgrown garden and the dry rustle of coin-shaped pods on a money plant. Two city workers on the corner labor over the new brick inlay for the sidewalk, making sure the angles fit together, part of a streetscape project meant to make the neighborhood walkable.

But on the inside, 400 Gorrell remains a vacant house on a vacant block. Only the walls tell the story, chapter by chapter, layer by layer—an archaeological dig through clashing wallpaper patterns and curtain rods nailed into plaster moldings.

In the big foyer, a round mirror is still set back in the wall where the engineer's wife might have checked her makeup before going to town. But there is no view from the third-floor turret anymore. Instead, a dropped ceiling somebody added, probably to save on heat, blocks the entrance.

Still intact in the dining room is a hand-carved ceiling, but the walls are papered with the women's pages from the old *Daily News*. Over the remnants of some raucous squatters' party, the faces of society matrons beam down serenely. "Mrs. Gregory Complimented at New Bern," says one headline. "Miss Whitner Says Vows with Dr. Bartlett," says another.

But that was in another life, and it has been a long time since anyone at this address made the society pages, or even the City Directory. By the 1990s, the residents at the big house on the corner of McAdoo were listed as *Not Verified*. By 1996, the description was simply *Vacant*.

Crime engulfed the neighborhood, bringing headlines nobody would paste up on the wall. The prostitutes who worked the bridge by the interstate started turning up dead. A seventy-five-year-old woman was raped. The neighborhood grocer was murdered in a robbery attempt up the block. Bennett women were accosted on their way to class. A couple was mugged at knifepoint while waiting for the bus.

Even the boarding houses could not make it, and the 1990 U.S. Census showed a third of the homes vacant. Of the people who remained, half lived in poverty, and 80 percent were renters paying less than $250 per month.

As rigor mortis set in, City Hall called for First Aid. With a committee report here, a public works project there, they patched and they mended. Finally, when all seemed lost, came an effort to fill the gaping hole in one fell swoop. But it was called SouthSide, not Gorrell Street. Because Gorrell Street had, as one historian told me, "such a bad connotation."

And we all know what a *connotation* is. It's the thing we think but don't say, and it's never a good thing. It's what grew up between us, after the old city lines weren't on paper anymore.

This was something harder to clear away than underbrush in the right-of-way and litter in the median. It's what makes people lock their car doors whenever they drive down a street, what makes a city give up on a neighborhood, until it almost seems too late. Until the day someone realizes that when we let the core rot, all that is left is a hollow shell.

Maybe you read the story in the paper on the "Ideas" page about how once-neglected urban neighborhoods around the country are coming back, now that people perceive crime as being down. And what a fine, hopeful idea that would be—just like the full-color SouthSide fliers that advertise "A Turn of the Century Neighborhood . . . Again."

So five years from now, when 400 Gorrell Street is a posh address once more, what urban pioneer will be living there? Will it be someone who saw what it had become, who cut back the tangled garden and cleaned up the Scorpion wine bottles and broken crack pipes?

Or will it be someone new, who doesn't know the old stories? Someone who stands on the corner and sees just a house, a fine old house, on a typical Southern street.

A longtime Greensboro metro columnist, **LORRAINE AHEARN** is the author of *The Man Who Became Santa Claus and Other Winter Tales*. Recipient of the national Casey Medal for Meritorious Journalism, she worked as a reporter for twenty-five years for Landmark Communications in Maryland and North Carolina. She teaches at Elon University and is a PhD candidate in media history at the University of North Carolina at Chapel Hill.

A Place Called Home

Ice

FRED CHAPPELL

BY 4:00 IN THE AFTERNOON the long bar of the Green Valley Grill is already beginning to crowd. A mid-February ice storm has brought down power lines in much of the western part of the city and people are seeking warmth, provender, and society. It is mostly an older group and a fair number of them have taken lodgings, filling the rooms of the O. Henry Hotel, the grand hostelry which houses the grill. The staff at the front desk is busily taking up telephone receivers — "We're sorry; we're all booked up for the next three days" — and cradling them again.

The seasoned residents of the city who could afford to reserve rooms had done so upon hearing the first reports of the approaching weather. Greensboro is prey to ice-storm visitations which can deprive certain sections of electric power for as long as a week. Houses sit dark and empty, except for pets which are tended by means of flashlight and lantern. For block after suburban block, all is deep shadow or thick darkness. The spooky silence is broken now and then by a dog's howl or by a strange, mournful human outcry that silences at once. The moon above the Starmount golf course seems touched with ice.

But the grill bar swarms with light and warmth and noise and the endless garish flicker of a television screen tuned to a sports channel no one is watching. The storm that has extinguished many a house light here ignites conversations a little more excited than usual, a little more disordered.

"Harry Fleming, where you been, partner? Haven't seen you since the Masters. Four years ago, was it?"

"Five."

"You haven't changed a bit. Still trim and fit. You must be doing well."

"Okay, I guess." . . . But in two minutes Harry reveals that he and Phyllis have split up, that she is living in Aspen with the guy who used to be Harry's superior at the brokerage, and that he has put their house on the market.

Jerry listens sympathetically. He had wanted to boast to his old acquaintance about his newly acquired skills with a sailboat. But now sail-boating seems an awkward subject to broach. He tells Harry that his son, Willard, barely squeaked through his first semester at East Carolina University and is considering dropping out. He may be shading the truth. Willard is a bright lad. Jerry follows a code of manners he could never describe or explain, but it enjoins him not to boast when his pal has struck upon ill fortune.

In the center booth four golfing buddies are seated at the round table, essaying humor about dentistry, a profession none of them follows.

"You talk about your broken tooth? I had to have my whole mouth replaced."

"What'd they replace it with, Gill?"

"The seventeenth hole of the Sedgefield course."

"Well, I wish you'd learn to hold your head still. My balls lip out on that one every time."

"Dumb joke. You owe me a beer."

"You're letting him off cheap, Jimbo. I'd fine him a case of scotch."

"Done."

The Atlantic Coast Conference basketball tournament is to be played in Greensboro this year. The opener is still some weeks off, but fringe personalities are already showing up. High school coaches, male and female, stand together, sipping short beers and gossiping in guarded tones. A couple of former college players sit at the bar, their heads prominent above those of the regular-sized men. Now and then the both of them sneak glances at the other patrons, trying to see if anyone has recognized them. An agent is easy to spot; he seems to have been placed in the scene by Central Casting. He is overweight, jowly, with thick eyebrows and heavily pomaded hair. As he talks to a young, mild-mannered, African American man—an assistant coach with a small college, perhaps—he chews methodically upon an unlit cigar. The object of his attention listens carefully, nodding at intervals. He does not speak.

Dishes begin to trot in from the kitchen. Everyone must have ordered at once and there follows a murmuring lull in the general babble as conversation is replaced with truffle fries, Darn Good Burgers, and occasional salads. The bartenders slide from place to place, watching the crowd at the bar without seeming to watch. The girls who serve the tables do not glide; they flutter cheerfully from spot to spot like butterflies investigating a pot garden. The music that chatter had submerged becomes audible. Ella Fitzgerald: "Love for Sale." No one listens. Maybe no one hears.

After an hour or so, those who have habitable homes go to inhabit them and are replaced by the dislodged. They drift in from the great dining hall for post-prandial coffee and liqueurs. Comfortable, turgid, perhaps too well fed, they seem resigned to their lot. Immersed within an easy ambience, they cannot claim to be discontent, yet would not admit to contentment. Here is a good place, probably the best possible at hand, but it is not home, nor even a "home away from home." It is a luxurious and expensive exile.

They do not take their comfortable situation for granted. They have lived in the world; they have suffered economic difficulties, familial tribulations, and maybe the cruelties of war. They are aware that employees of the power company are stalking about in the cold, trying to defend themselves from black ice, arc flash, from the uncertainly illuminated false step, and from trees that ice has fashioned into spears and daggers. The patrons are grateful for their safety and well-being, but they are unsatisfied.

From time to time the faces of those standing at the bar light up in a startling way, glowing as white as clown faces in the glare of their iPhone screens. Then they mutter rapidly or thumb furiously, catching at hints and giblets of intelligence from the world abroad. It seems that what they receive merely confirms what they had already presumed to know, for they shake their heads with regret and tuck the gadgets away. Occasionally one of them smiles and snaps the screen shut and heads down the long corridor to the elevators in the main lobby. Maybe this man is going to repack his bags; maybe heat and light have been returned to Lindley Park or Glenwood or Sunset Hills. A new energy informs his gait as he treads the silent carpet.

The sports agent speaking to the young coach at the bar has made no progress. He tries again to buy the young man another bourbon, but he declines and shakes his head repeatedly. He is turning down whatever propositions are being offered. When he shifts his gaze to the other end of the bar, he recognizes an acquaintance and strides toward his friend, careful to say his name. "Didn't think I'd see *you* here, Walter." The agent blinks, chews the cigar, takes a notepad from the inner pocket of his suit jacket, and makes a note with a silver ballpoint. Then he begins to watch the TV, where Kansas State and Louisville are trading baskets.

As a middle booth empties, it is refilled by a family, father and mother in their sixties, son and wife in their thirties. They are conversing even as they seat themselves, carrying on with a subject broached at table in the dining hall. The mother engages her son earnestly and intensely. The father places his hand on his wife's forearm to gentle her mood. The daughter-in-law seems to wish she were seated within a different continent. When the server arrives, she has to stand by patiently while the mother makes a final, most telling point.

Seated across from each other at one of the small tables at the west wall, two teenagers, brother and sister, by the looks of them, are rapidly fingering laptops. Are they competing in a video game? Their eyes are fixed, their lips tight. Now and then the boy, the younger sibling, crows in triumph and his sister gives him a look of utter disgust. No human specimen before his time has ever received such a loathing regard. When their mother comes to gather them to Room 512, bedtime, her son tries to chronicle for her his evening of many victories. She ignores him studiously.

The sports agent at the bar engages his old-fashioned cell phone, reading in muted tones from the notes he took down earlier. He pauses, listens for a longish spell, nods, and clicks off. Too bad. Better luck next time.

The hour grays toward closing time. The bar crew begins to tidy and tot up. A man in his sixties who has sat alone for an hour orders a nightcap. The barman questions him briefly, then sets out an espresso with a Remy on the side. He also delivers the tab, and the solitary awkwardly extracts four twenties from his billfold.

The lights are dimmed; the kitchen is quieting. Sonny Rollins renders a slow version of " 'Round Midnight."

What if the hotel went dark? What if the generators failed, and the secondary systems also? What might we see in these immense, hushed, daunting spaces?

Nothing at first.

Then, eyes. Eyes peering inside through the plate-glass doors, through the west windows, through the patio windows.

The eyes of dogs and coyotes, of homeless men and injured women, of lost children. Eyes of a distant land. They do not judge. They only observe with persistent and weary patience. They do not blink.

In 2004, **FRED CHAPPELL** retired after forty years in the English department at the University of North Carolina at Greensboro. He has published more than two dozen books of poetry (most recently *Familiars*), fiction, and critical commentary. His latest novel, *Shadow Master Astolfo,* will be published in 2015. He has received numerous awards for his work, and served as North Carolina Poet Laureate for five years.

The Hunted

QUINN DALTON

WE LIVE APPROXIMATELY three thousand feet, as the crow flies, from a pair of tigers, Axl and Kisa. Ten-year-old siblings born in captivity and hand-raised, they now reside in the Animal Discovery Zoo at the Greensboro Science Center.

I love them.

The day I fell in love with them was not long after they arrived, when my daughters were six and two. It was a quiet afternoon at the science center, not many people around. As I wheeled Alia toward the enclosure, Avery trotting along beside me, Axl looked up at us from where he was lounging maybe fifty feet away. His sister was lying diva-on-a-piano style on the high rocks at the far end of the enclosure. She raised her head a bit higher to regard us, maybe sensing her brother's interest, then settled back into cool repose. Axl meanwhile kept his gaze on us.

A sort of thrill ran through me that we'd claimed his attention. Then he was up, as if he'd never been down, and he ran—no, not ran; that's too simple—he gathered and burst or flew straight toward us, stopping hard at the high fence. I stopped hard too. Avery squeezed my hand. He watched us go past him into the three-sided glass observation nook. He strolled back and forth in front of the glass. The girls were ecstatic that he was sticking so close, Alia clapping her hands and Avery patting the glass.

But my skin was prickling, the muscles in my legs twitching. I thought of Axl's steady, appraising stare.

This was what it felt like to be prey.

The girls soon wanted to move on—there were, after all, goats you could pet. I thought of what Axl could do with one of those in five minutes. I could've stayed there all day watching him and his sister.

On our way to the petting zoo, we passed a docent. I wheeled Alia over to her, Avery following along. I asked the tigers' names. "We got quite a welcome from Axl just now," I said.

She looked down at the stroller and my squirming daughter. "Oh, they often come running when they see strollers."

Yep, we were food. Nothing breaks it down simpler than that. All your thoughts about yourself and who you are, all the trappings of your life, all your ideas about the world and your place in it—well, they don't seem so clear cut, so present anymore.

Maybe that's why I fell in love with them. My beautiful daughters were young and I was their favorite person in the world. I had been happily married for about a decade. I was working my eyeballs out. I loved my life, but a lot of it had been figured out, as far as I could tell. I didn't feel caged exactly, just that I could see the edges of things.

I didn't want to escape, or be eaten by a tiger. I just wanted to be looked at in a new way, in a way I couldn't recognize and categorize and negotiate with. This was what it felt like to be looked at by Axl and Kisa. Their raw beauty, their slow-motion stroll, more like swimming than walking, their skin like liquid over their muscles, their eyes another liquid I could never name. I wanted to be seen. I wanted to be seen by them.

Axl and Kisa were two years old and weighed a respective four hundred and three hundred pounds when they arrived at the science center in 2006. Their mother was one of a number of big cats rescued from a facility in

Ohio that had racked up hundreds of animal welfare violations. Some of the big cats were relocated to the Conservator's Center in rural Caswell County. The staff had not known initially that Axl and Kisa's mother was pregnant. Axl and Kisa were her secret. They were later transferred to the Greensboro Science Center on permanent loan.

The siblings are most likely a mix of Bengal and Amur (Siberian). They're considered of generic breed, and because of this they won't ever become parents themselves. Axl has a vasectomy, but this doesn't stop him from making an effort when Kisa is in estrus.

And yes, that is something to see—seven hundred pounds of combined tiger going at it for about five to ten seconds, teeth bared and growling. Whenever I've seen this, my favorite thing is to look around at any other parents who have up until that moment been exhorting their children to pay attention, to quit slapping their sister or whatever, and to *look*.

Their interest seems to fall off sharply once Axl climbs aboard. At that point, people tend to scatter. I find that hilarious. One woman told her child the animals were playing leapfrog. When my daughter began to helpfully correct her on the matter, I steered her away, much as a tigress might cuff her cub back from a coiling snake.

And this is where we have to face how we impose our worldview even on animals that could catch and debone us without too much effort.

Another time I saw Kisa fighting Axl off—his timing was bad apparently; she was no longer in heat. I stood with my kids in the enclosure, watching Kisa keeping Axl at bay. She had thrown herself down, back against the fence, all plate-sized paws up, claws and teeth at the ready.

A couple was standing next to us in the enclosure. The man turned to his wife and said, "Is he doing what I think he's doing?"

The woman caught my eye. I shrugged. "They're brother and sister," I said. "But pickings are slim."

The woman eyed me, then looked at her husband. "Men," she said.

Of the two, Axl is said to be the more affectionate one, affectionate being a relative term when you're dealing with an animal that weighs nearly a quarter ton and has four-inch incisors—the longest of all the big cats. But what this means is that he's more social, making himself available when the keepers want him to be. He's more game for training—more willing to come out in the morning when it's time to "go to work" and then, in the evening, to come back into their protected enclosure.

Kisa by contrast is more reticent and apprehensive, and at times, a bit smug. I've been told Kisa seems to be well aware that she's still going to get fed no matter what she does, so she's rarely in a hurry to do as she's asked.

To this, some people might say, "Women."

She teases her brother sometimes, sneaking up on him and biting his ankles, but she also knows when to give him space—a good thing since he outweighs her by a hundred pounds.

They eat a prescribed diet comprised of vitamin-fortified horse, beef, and organ meat every afternoon at four. In the summer heat, when they're less active, Axl might consume about six pounds and Kisa three; in the winter when the cold air sparks their Siberian spirits, they might eat as much as twelve and eight pounds, respectively.

Occasionally one of the maintenance staff, a hunter, brings them treats—rabbit, portions of venison.

Other treats they get during training consist of horse, chicken, or pork chunks. And no, they're not jumping through hoops of fire or being saddled up—this is training to make possible the health maintenance of massive animals that could flay you with one swipe. They have learned to sit, lie down, open their mouths for inspection (learning in Kisa's case, of course, may not necessarily translate to doing). They've been taught to "present" various body parts if shots or other care is needed— shoulders, paws, ears—against a heavy-duty fence. At one time, for example, Axl had to present his ear for regular cleanings after Kisa nailed him during a fight.

They love snow; they love their pool. Kisa keeps to the rocks mostly; Axl likes to pace the perimeter of the one-acre enclosure. You can almost hear the change jingling in his pockets.

Why do I mention these day-to-day trivialities? Because they're meaningful to me. Maybe for the same reason one wants to know more about one's favorite musician or author—I'm a fan. I want to know what makes Axl and Kisa who they are. As a human, I can't help but want to know them in some way, or feel like I do. I want to understand how they live in this world.

Another visit, a couple of years later. Alia no longer needs the stroller as we follow the winding path to visit Axl and Kisa. Alia holds my hand; Avery walks a few feet ahead, already showing me her separate—her Kisa—nature.

There are no other visitors—at least that's how I remember it. As we near the enclosure, both tigers rush to us this time, a gold and black blur, and then with just the same blinding energy, they're still as stone, watching us.

On the one hand, how exciting to get this double greeting. The kids yell with pleasure, while the cats flirt with us from their side of the fence, come-hither looks over their shoulders as they pace past us and then bring themselves around.

But some deep, low-brain doom spreads through me, shortening my breath. I bring the kids into the glass enclosure while the cats take turns rubbing the corners of the glass walls. I see a docent walking by; I can't leave my kids in that space and I can't herd them fast enough to catch up to her, so I call out an "Excuse me!"

The docent strolls over. "You know," I say, "when we walked up, Axel and Kisa ran right over to us. I know someone said they like strollers, but I was just curious . . ."

I trail off as the docent glances at my young daughters and then back at me. She says, "No, they just like them that size."

I think I say thank you. I know I keep my hands on both of my girls, who by now are fidgeting, wanting to see the maned wolves, the meerkats, the tortoises. I hold them still anyway for a moment, wishing they had scruffs I could easily pinch. We watch Axl and Kisa pace, hear the low rumbles in their throats.

All the love, all the late-night feedings, all the kisses I had covered my daughters with—so shocked I was at the physical nature of my love for them—come down to this. Flesh and blood. Predator and prey. I allow myself to feel the terror of what it would be like to be pursued by these creatures. My body tingles, my breath goes shallow, my body aches to make a run for it. Would I be able to save my children? Would my offspring prevail?

What can I say? I'm a writer; I obsess over the unknown, the odd, things that most likely could never come to pass—the *what if*.

There are the normal worries we try to keep at bay by looking both ways, buckling our seat belts, locking our doors at night, swiftly crossing a dark parking lot. But all the ways I was taught to look out for myself—all these flimsy precautions come to ash in the low fire of these animals' gazes.

Maybe it's the way they flatten all other fears—maybe that's what claims me.

The fact that they live in the heart of this Piedmont city never ceases to impress me—and fill me with some kind of wild joy as well. In winter from certain vantages in Country Park, which backs up to their enclosure, you can see them flickering among the bare woods. With the dark fence blurred to invisibility, it's as if they're just strolling among our pines, oaks, and maples, as foreign as a pair of dinosaurs.

They are one of the wonders of our town.

They thrive in a home our science center made—and the center itself is a jewel we Greensboro folks can be proud of. Part museum, part zoo, and now aquarium, it holds a rare dual certification from the Association of Zoos and Aquariums and the American Alliance of Museums. Sorry to verge into brochure copy here, but it's a big deal. We did good, and a good many of us have made it happen, with our faithful memberships and visits, our donations, our community support across otherwise hard-drawn political lines.

What do Axl and Kisa think about us? I'm trapped in my human self and so I can't help but ask the question. Of course the answer is probably, well, nothing. But they see us. They see us looking at them. They smell us; they regard us in their impassive, calculating, heart-stopping cool. A few times they have looked straight at me, and thrilled me to my soul.

We can't explain what we love—well maybe some things, but not everything. Why am I drawn to them? I've tried to understand it but the question still feels unanswered. Maybe I will never answer it. All I know is that their presence tugs at me, a gravitational pull. In truth, in this world, they are the hunted, but they hunt me, too.

Before I knew that even a tiger's roar doesn't carry that far, before I knew they are locked safely away each night, I used to stand in my front yard after my daughters were tucked in their beds, and I listened for them, believing I would be more likely to hear them when the traffic on Lawndale died down and when they shifted into nocturnal alertness.

I've heard the howler monkeys before. Believe me, those whoops get my dog's attention. But never a roar from my tiger idols, not so much as a rumble from across the road.

Nevertheless. Sometimes I stand outside at night, listening anyway.

QUINN DALTON is the author of a novel, *High Strung*, and two story collections, *Bulletproof Girl* and *Stories from the Afterlife*. Her short stories, essays, and articles on the writing craft have appeared in publications such as *Glimmer Train, One Story, Poets & Writers, Mediabistro.com*, and *New Stories from the South: The Year's Best*. Her new novel, *Curve of My Heart*, is forthcoming next year.

On a Rocky Inland Coast

LEE ZACHARIAS

I CAME TO GREENSBORO from the Ozark Mountains in Arkansas and to Arkansas from the Blue Ridge Mountains of Virginia. For a couple of years before that I lived in Richmond, with its then thriving downtown and the tumbling rapids of the James River, in a funky urban neighborhood called the Fan, the ocean a short two-hour drive away. And before that? Let's just say that for the twenty-five years that led up to my move south, I was a Midwesterner longing to escape the bland flatlands and ranch houses of my youth.

I arrived in Greensboro, never having seen it, in August of 1975. That past winter I had accepted a teaching job at the University of North Carolina at Greensboro over the phone, the only job I could get without a campus interview. UNCG had interviewed me in December, at the annual Modern Language Association conference in New York. There, a UNCG professor sent to entertain me in the hotel hall while I waited for the interview told me how much I would like Greensboro because there were hardly any bars, everyone went to church, the neighborhoods were all

clean and new, and it was a great place to raise a family. At the time I had
no children, was in the process of divorcing my first husband, and every
virtue he named seemed a demerit to me.

The interview went no better. The department head never looked up as
he read course descriptions from the college catalog and asked only one
question: How many could I teach? I thought I'd rather crawl into a coffin
than move to Greensboro. But then a bad flu turned into pneumonia on
a bone-chilling, rainy January night in New Orleans, where I had gone for
my first on-site interview at Tulane, and I was out for the season. I didn't
choose Greensboro; it chose me.

And so that August I set out from Arkansas with a carsick puppy beside
me on the front seat of a twenty-four-foot U-Haul and all my worldly
goods rattling around the back because the ten-foot truck I'd reserved had
transmission problems and the bigger truck was the best the office could
do. It was evening by the time I backed it down my mountain driveway
and into a ditch, night by the time I reached I-40, where I discovered that
all the motels from Fort Smith to North Carolina were full. I spent my one
night on the road trying to doze on the front seat with my head in a pool of
puppy vomit at a truck stop outside of Little Rock; and near midnight the
next day, I rolled into Greensboro, wanting nothing more than a shower
and a beer. I drove for miles before I found an open convenience store.
It was 12:05 on a Saturday night (or Sunday morning, depending on how
you mark time), and there was a big sign on the cooler that said *No Alcohol
Sales After Midnight*. Arkansas had no Sunday sales either, but we were near
the Oklahoma border, and on central time back in Fayetteville there were
fifty-five minutes left before the drive-thru window of the package store
went dark.

The 7-Eleven was the second disappointment of the night, because
I had hoped that Greensboro might be in the mountains, in the foothills at
least. It was dark by the time I passed Asheville and braked my way down
Black Mountain, but I could feel the land unroll beneath me. Indeed, when

I woke the next morning, I was in the flatlands again, and before anyone objects let me say that while Greensboro appears hilly to those who arrive from the coast, it most decidedly does not to anyone driving in from the mountains. I looked for a river. The downtown was in its last stages of decay, and the ocean a long two hundred miles away. My Renault, which had been driven by a friend (who was supposed to drive the truck, but that's another story), had broken down on the trip and needed parts that never seemed to come. Students had claimed all the rental property near the university, and the one place I toured that would allow pets was a cramped duplex overlooking the city's water treatment plant. I spent most of my first semester commuting from an apartment near Guilford College on a bus that had only one scheduled run in the morning and another in the afternoon, and though logic tells me it can't possibly have rained every day, the details of memory are stubborn. What I recall is waiting for the inevitably late bus in a downpour that lasted three months.

"It's just a year," my boyfriend and I assured each other when he arrived. "A year and that's it." We missed the built-in community of grad school, where we had met. He commuted to adjunct teaching at Elon College; and out in the suburban land of no sidewalks, no friends, and not one street that could be crossed safely on foot, both of us felt stranded. We were writers, we'd come up through the Sixties, we were rebels, for God's sake, and compared to the rough edge of the Ozarks, Greensboro seemed overly civilized.

Yet here we are thirty-nine years later. What we found was a community of talented, accomplished, and unpretentious writers, quite unlike the posturing, competitive writing community we had come from. My then boyfriend, now my husband of thirty-two years, taught another year at Elon, then for fourteen at Bennett College, before moving on to finish his career at High Point University. Even before he retired he found another calling in hospice, and for the past dozen years he has been a volunteer for one of the best chapters in the nation. Midway through our second year we bought a little house in Latham Park, and on its screened porch I finished my first novel, which paid for the big old barn where we still live in Sunset Hills. In it we raised a son, we are part of a neighborhood, our dog patrols its sidewalks, we have friends throughout the city. The downtown underwent a renaissance and is now thriving. And I found my way to Ocracoke Island, where for the past twenty-five years I have spent as much of May as I can. Its wildness, marshes, forests, and long stretch of untamed beach are my church.

But each time I returned from the island, as we sat on our back deck gazing out over the azaleas, I would say, "Well, it's not Ocracoke, but it's not bad." No matter how welcoming, there's not much a community can do to change its location, to build a mountain range or import a shoreline.

Until the storm.

My husband was en route to visit a friend in Detroit the day our landscape changed. I had been doing yard work—by then I had a lovely flower garden along the back fence in addition to the vegetable patch behind the garage—and was standing on the side deck chatting with a neighbor when I saw the wall of black approaching. My son was in a class at Grimsley High School when he looked out the window. "Holy shit!" he exclaimed and was promptly sent to detention as the teacher slammed the shade down and attempted to go on with the lesson.

What I said was "I'd better close the garage," though by the time I reached it I was running. I made it back to the deck and was just though the door when glass began to shatter, the wind tore off gutters along with part of our roof, and trees began to topple. The largest of several we lost was a maple in the center of the backyard that split in three directions. "Holy shit," my son said again when he came home at lunch and opened the gate to find me in a backyard full of downed hardwood. I phoned ahead to my husband's friend and said, "Tell him to call home when he gets there. We've had a tornado." It was not, according to the meteorologists, who called it a microburst, even a gust-nado, but as I say memory is stubborn.

The stump that was left when tree surgeons cleaned up the mess was ninety-three inches across. Because the stump grinders were so backlogged, I had an entire summer to contemplate the hole it would leave behind. I didn't know that the stump grinder leaves a mini-mountain rather than a hole, but this was at the height of the water-garden craze, and I figured that if I could not live beside a mountain stream or at the ocean, I would build my own coast right in my backyard.

The grinders left their hill, but I was unfazed. I hired two teenagers to dig. They were school dropouts, who wore T-shirts advertising their band Pugnacious Bastards and whose every other word to me was "please" or "thank you." These were boys who never bathed, and whenever one entered the house it was an effort not to gag, but I've never hired better or more honest workers.

The yard was nearly impossible to dig, given the massive tree roots spread beneath the baked brick of heavy clay soil, but the Pugnacious Bastards persisted. Where roots as dense as petrified wood protruded into the growing hole, they terraced underwater shelves for plants. Of my flower garden these two beautiful, unwashed boys who would go on to rough times said, "It's so pretty. Would you mind if we just sat here for a minute to look?" Every break they took they insisted upon deducting from their wages, and I winced at the inked thumbprints on the cancelled checks, because what those prints said was that they had no bank accounts, no home in the civilized world, they were institutionally suspect. As for the pond, they got so carried away that the center is more than waist deep, and I had to order a custom liner because the largest one available would not fit.

I bought a ton of rocks to line its shore, and then another to build a waterfall. Over the years I've added at least two more tons—some I've purchased, some were given by a friend who later killed himself, some I've picked up on my travels. There are lava rocks from Costa Rica, cobbles from the Côte d'Azur, small boulders from the Tennessee River, pebbles worn smooth by the waves of Lake Michigan up in Michigan's north woods, others I no longer remember pocketing. I added plants, including a yellow iris that has spread throughout the yard, two water lilies, and the underwater oxygenators recommended by the books. My bright koi, fantails, and shubunkins felt so at home that I fed them only once before they recognized my footstep and swam to the side, thrusting their mouths up out of the water to nibble from my hand. Dragonflies rested on the reeds. Wasps dipped their heads from their narrow waists to drink. In winter from the second-story window of my study I watched crows skate across the ice over and over, buoyed by the happy babble of their caws. In the summer my mother loved sitting out on a bench to observe the robins, cardinals, titmice, and sparrows bathe and splash. Our older son, my stepson, and I spent hours of his visits on that same bench, seeking Ghost Fish, a small, elusive second-generation gray shadow darting beneath the lilies. Nature frolicked.

Nature exploded.

What you learn when you attend its church is that the serpent does not invade the garden. The serpent *is* the garden.

The fantails were the first to die, followed by Roy the Koi, named by our younger son, but the shubunkins were so hardy they soon became enormous. They were also prolific breeders, so well fed they had no need to eat their own fry. I started with eleven fish and soon had a bio-overload of more than two hundred. I cut off the food supply and let nature take its course.

Even so, filtration was a problem. Every other week I had to crawl under a thorny rose bush to unplug and move half a ton of rocks to expose the heavy, drum-shaped above-ground filter, drag it over to the grass and hose it down, move more rocks to pull out the clogged pump and jet-spray the muck. The accordion material inside the filter swelled, and it became harder and harder to reassemble and seal. I bought the expensive UV sterilizer recommended by the experts, which required a second pump to clean, but still the water clouded, and when the weather warmed the next spring

I was out there swirling a toilet brush, trying in vain to collect the veils of bright green algae. I built a biofilter that worked like magic — overnight the water grew so clear you could toss in a penny and read the date off the bottom, until one day early the next spring, that is, when I stepped into the backyard to find my fish struggling to swim at the bottom of a mudhole. The biofilter, the whiskey-barrel–sized rubber tub I had filled with pebbles and plants and buried beneath the waterfall — a waterfall I've rebuilt, rock by rock, well over a dozen times now — was bulging with the expanding roots of the plants, and the water from my pond was leaking over the back and sides. I took it apart, rinsed batch after batch of pebbles in a kitchen colander and put it back together again, this time with a single plant, but even that one plant grew such vigorous roots that the first warm day of the next spring my pond drained itself again.

I gave up on the biofilter and found a packet of crystals billed as a natural water clarifier. It too worked like magic, and for easy refills I anchored the plastic dispenser beneath a flagstone with six-pound test line, though of course the line broke and the dispenser disappeared. After that I just threw the packets in, which worked fine until Lowe's stopped stocking them. For a year or two I bought them online, but then the retail source disappeared from the web, though I could still get them if I really wanted — all I would have to do is open a dealership.

These days when I spy a great blue heron crossing our yard as I sit writing upstairs I no longer reach for my camera but beat on the window, shouting, "You leave my fish alone!" Neighborhood cats took care of the fish in the other pond I installed early on to serve as an isolation ward for a fish who seemed sick but turned out to be pregnant. But even though that pond has long since been filled in and the big pond is deep enough for the remaining fish to elude them, the cats love to scamper about the edges, chasing birds, overturning potted plants, knocking rocks and statuary in.

The two lilies that turned out to be a waxy white instead of deep pink overgrew by the second year and began climbing the rocks like kudzu, their roots so stubbornly wrapped around the stones on the bottom that I had to hire a man to pry them out and start over with a new lily. However, even a single lily will overgrow in the second year, I've discovered, and I am perpetually in the market for muscle. Except for the iris, most of the marginal plants died the first winter, but the oxygenators proved so invasive that at times my little paradise looked more like an overdressed salad than a pond. It took me years to rid myself of them.

Have I mentioned the magnolia tree with its steady rain of leathery leaves and pods? Or the wisteria, the wild grapevine, and clematis that come up through the rocks to climb the nandina forest I planted behind? The morning glories brought by birds? This year I dug up the nandinas, so that I can at least spot the vines and spray them when they sprout, a technique that does not work in the garden of day lilies and annuals I planted to mimic the pond's curve.

In short I discovered that maintaining a pond in one's backyard is about as much trouble as maintaining a vacation home in the mountains or at the coast.

But there it is, a little heaven that contains its own hell but is much too big for me to take out. These days my husband and I rarely sit out to share a drink before dinner. When we do he complains of the bugs, and while the fish take care of the mosquito larvae and the yard is no buggier than anyone else's, the dog won't rest until he coaxes someone to play ball. Instead we watch the news or take pause on the screened porch. Even so the pond offers both of us moments of respite as deep as its reflections, the crabapple blossoms in early spring, the moon late at night, even the sharp white pitch of the garage against a gloss of blue sky. The most ordinary things are made miracles inside its mirrored pool, and to watch the fish swimming about is as calming and restorative as the practice of yoga. There is a history piled in its rocks and sunk below its surface, those weeks of grace given to those boys who dug it and then came back to sit beside it when it was filled, the dragonflies, the birds, the wasps, the family members, some gone, others distant, the friend we still miss who brought us the rocks from the Tennessee River; a present and a future in the delight of a neighbor's grandchild as she scatters food for those otherwise self-sufficient fish. And in the trickle of water over stone each time I return from the mountains or the coast I hear its message: *listen*, it whispers, *you are home.*

LEE ZACHARIAS, emerita professor of English at the University of North Carolina at Greensboro, is the author of a collection of short stories and two novels. She is the recipient of grants from the National Endowment for the Arts and the North Carolina Arts Council, North Carolina's Sir Walter Raleigh Award for Fiction, and other awards. Her nonfiction has been reprinted in *The Best American Essays*. Her most recent book is *The Only Sounds We Make,* a collection of personal essays.

Why I Live Where I Live

JOHN L. ROBINSON

"THERE'S AN ALLIGATOR IN THE BIG LAKE," she shouted as we jogged past each other on the trail. She was, it is probably worth noting, running away from the lake.

There were two issues in her comment. First, the lake isn't exactly big. Calling this a *big* lake is like calling Lake Jeanette the Atlantic Ocean. It's called the big lake simply because it is larger than the other three bodies of water in the neighborhood we grandly call lakes.

Second, an alligator? In a little lake in Greensboro?

I was dubious, but not disbelieving. My home is in suburbia, less than four miles from downtown, but wildlife is surprisingly abundant, thanks to smart city planners and developers sixty or seventy years ago. A creek bordered on both sides by woods and walking trails cuts a narrow swath through the subdivision. Yet that, along with the lakes, attract enough fauna to stock a traveling petting zoo.

I run the trail before dawn, and I'm not embarrassed to admit that it can get spooky. Once, as I was loping along, deep in a daydream, screams shattered the quiet and brought me to a dead stop. There was a moment of silence, and the whoops and cries broke the silence again. It sounded as if a child, maybe two, were crying out in pain. I looked around, trying to determine what direction they were coming from. Then I realized they were the screams of a two barred owls. Or maybe just one. Whatever, the racket made my skin crawl.

Another time on a predawn run, the woods rustled to my right. It was too dark for me to see clearly, but it sounded as if I was being followed. I quickened my pace, and the noise tracked me. I couldn't think of any good reason why someone would be following me. But it couldn't be good. No one was going to pop out of the woods at 5 a.m. to give me a Publishers Clearing House check.

Instead, what emerged about ten yards up the trail were four deer, which trotted into the trees on the other side. At least, I think they were deer. Yes, I'm sure they were.

Still, that doesn't compete with the time when I was working in the front yard of a house about a mile away, and a deer complete with antlers trotted down the middle of the street for a full block, calm as Mariano Rivera, walking out in the ninth inning to save yet another Yankees' win.

Our house abuts a pond—it's actually considered one of the four lakes, but it's small compared with the *big* lake. (I can throw a rock across the pond to my neighbor's yard; not that I ever have, Bob.) Yet it's enough to attract a heron to come and fish. Or the hawk that hunts the same habitat. He sits on a tree branch about twenty feet from our window, ominously overlooking the grounds. People fish in the pond, too, but they're more likely to catch a turtle. I've seen some with shells the size of hubcaps and heads the size of my fist.

I write less fondly about the geese, which turn us into amateur Lil Bucks, jookin' to avoid the goose poop. I admit to getting a measure of satisfaction watching the local swan—yes, we have swans, too—jab at a goose when it comes too close. While the geese outnumber the swan, it's clear the swan's attitude is "You're many and I'm but one, but I'm going to take out four or five of you before you get me . . . so, who's first?" The geese always back off.

But a gator? Could it be that one of the mythical babies brought back as a pet from Florida and flushed down the toilet has grown to adulthood in the sewers of Greensboro? Could it feed on the little dogs that are walked around the pond?

When I approached the big lake, dawn was still about thirty minutes away, and the light was dim. A group of four or five people stood along the banks, about two hundred yards away. By the time I had reached where they were, they had dispersed. But looking down, I saw that there was, in fact, an alligator, gray and about six feet long, lying motionless in the water.

"What the hell?" I thought as I recklessly stepped forward. It didn't move, but it seemed to be eyeing me. I stepped back. I watched for another moment, not seeing any kind of movement—no breathing, no twitch, no blink—but what do I know about gators? Maybe they can float motionless for hours.

Then a ripple passed and the gator bobbed. And continued bobbing in time with the ripples. I laughed. Someone had put a hard plastic alligator in the lake, presumably to attract gullible people like me. #winning!

I ran on, pleased I live in a place where man, nature, and plastic toys coexist. About a hundred yards later, another jogger approached, heading toward the lake.

"There's an alligator in the big lake," I shouted as we passed. And I smiled.

A twenty-nine-year Greensboro resident, **JOHN L. ROBINSON** is the former editor of the *News & Record* and now teaches journalism and mass communication at the University of North Carolina at Chapel Hill. He roams around the Starmount Forest and Hamilton Lakes neighborhoods.

Losing Ground

VALERIE NIEMAN

Dunkard Mill Run: The Farm

1

Forest once-upon-a.
Deer chestnut turkey bear ginseng oak squirrel berry. Once.
Then saws and axes made great trees human-size.
Cabin into house, scratched plot to fields, to industrial
drifts of hogs battening on the trash of hotel kitchens.
Later, the ground was in hay. Timothy and foxtail.
Wind stroked the hill's long flanks.

2

We built a house and made a new garden:
bowls and bones came up with each shovel turn.
I grew corn and cantaloupe, beans and tomatoes.
Dug deep to plant orchards, though
not deep enough to root the marriage.

3

The first year, stunned by loneliness,
I sowed but didn't tend.
The next summer, volunteer tomatoes
struggled against pigweed. By the time

witchgrass overran the strawberries
and the raspberries crumbled from virus,
I was gone, too.

4
I expect my apples still bear faithfully:
Lodi Macoun Spy and Winesap.
Asparagus will last decades,
but apples are for generations.
Until forest.

Greensboro, North Carolina: The Women

Snowdene lived all her married years and then her widowed years in the little white house on Elam. She planted spider lilies, four o'clocks, Spanish bells, snow on the mountain. When she put down her trowel, I came along to pick it up. Finding, freeing, lifting, and replanting, I was Bingham at Machu Picchu, Carter in Egypt, rediscovering the old.

I planted irises brought from West Virginia: yellow flags from a swale on the farm, bronze giants whose knotty rhizomes had been passed to me by a mountain woman. I planted lilies of the valley that my mother had carried from state to state to state.

One day, on a cut-across street, I saw a sign by a cottage: "Ditch lilies, dig all you want."

An old woman sat on the porch as I lifted clumps of orange trumpets. All you want, she said. With years of growth and spread, they had choked themselves and needed new ground.

In the summer sun I spaded up baskets of lilies to plant on Elam, where I lived solitary and then lived married at that little white house.

Leawood Drive: Lilies

1

Did they survive our December move?

2

I waited for spring.
Double River Wye spiked up
and blossomed, along with nameless
others, white, mango, golden-throat, grape.
Year by year I set out new additions:
Children's Festival, Coney Island, Old King Cole.
The last I planted were lemon lilies,
Hemerocallis flava, fragrant sister
to those hoyden ditch lilies.

3

June 5.
I backed down the driveway.
White Orientals trumpeted
by the mailbox, and Happy Returns shone
with sunny promises not to be kept.

4

Each night at the edge of uneasy sleep,
I imagined the unfolding show—
blossoms opening and fading
without my witness,
still, I know how the lilies increase,
roots fattening in the clay.

Somewhere to Go

Attachment is the cause of pain, but then, the Buddha was no gardener.

From Leawood I took what could be carried: a red rose in a green pot, a basket of strawberries. The scrabbly burr-rose from Elam, lifted again, roots (for a time) in sandy soil at my parents' home.

I cannot let go.

Not of any, not of a life lived by growing and tending. Not of the lilies of the valley moved and moved, not of the silvery money plant, seeded and reseeded. Not the lilies, not the iris, not the striped camellia I blessed each morning. Not even the pink phlox straggling beside the road where once I stood to catch the school bus. Even that.

I fly home and home and home.

"Losing Ground" will appear in **VALERIE NIEMAN**'s second poetry book, *Hotel Worthy*. Her most recent novel, *Blood Clay*, earned the 2012 Eric Hoffer Prize in General Fiction. She has held fellowships from the National Endowment for the Arts and the North Carolina Arts Council. An alumna of West Virginia University and Queens University of Charlotte, she was a journalist before becoming a professor at NC A&T State University.

Ellen and the Great Trees

ANN DEAGON

IT WAS NO WONDER ELLEN thought we worshipped trees. And maybe we did. Our younger daughter Ellen was born without the capacity to understand language. Of necessity, being extremely intelligent, she relied on her senses to try to make sense of the world. She read our faces and our motions, shared our routines, our pleasures, our sorrows. She perceived, sooner than we did, how trees lay at the center of our life.

When my husband and I first came to teach at Guilford College in 1956, the great Revolutionary Oak, under which the Quakers had buried men who died at the Battle of Guilford Courthouse in 1781, still lay on the ground in New Garden cemetery, brought down by a bomb set at its roots to explode as Eleanor Roosevelt spoke at the college to an integrated audience. Behind the cemetery a path runs down through the woods, where escaped slaves would wait to board the Underground Railroad, down to a tree-lined street, Woodbrook Drive. We built our home there in 1960.

Three giant beech trees overlook the house, along with shag-bark hickories, holly trees, and various evergreens. Every Christmas we would drive our van into the college woods and cut down a cedar tree tall enough to touch our twelve-foot ceiling. We would decorate it with lights, glass balls, strings of gold-painted pine cones, and an angel on top. Underneath we'd set all the children's dolls in their cradles — and Ellen herself as a baby was in her Cherokee basket among them. We would sing carols on

Christmas Eve, and of course in the morning there would be new toys and gifts under the tree.

In good weather the neighborhood children would gather under the beech tree in the center of the back yard, home base for their games of tag and hide-and-seek. The child who was "it" would cross arms against the trunk, hide her face, and count to one hundred while the others scattered behind the trees and outbuildings. We adults never thought of these rituals as religious, but one evening we noticed Ellen take to her bed a picture book entitled *Now I Lay Me Down to Sleep,* whose cover showed a little boy kneeling beside his bed with his head in his arms. She knelt that way, and we wondered what on earth would come out of her mouth. She said: "Five, ten, fifteen, twenty." We have been told that God is a number, and Ellen had that number down!

It was not only in the fall, when the hickory nuts rained down on our roof, or winter, when we gathered kindling and cut logs for the fireplaces, or spring, when birds and squirrels were nesting in the trees and hawks hunting—but also in summer we would set out cross country sleeping in the wooded campgrounds and national forests, where once we saw on a great trunk higher than we could reach the claw marks of a grizzly bear. In California we gathered pine cones from unfamiliar species, and once drove our van right through a giant hollow redwood tree. And down from the home of a beloved former student we came upon what they call a redwood cathedral—a circle of tall redwoods that had sprung up just outside the round shadow of the mother tree, itself now gone for centuries. Holy ground.

All ground is holy, and all that springs from that ground. That's what Ellen knew without words, and what I try to give word to while I live.

I am Ann Deagon, and these are my words.

ANN DEAGON's poetry collections are *Carbon 14, Poetics South, There Is No Balm in Birmingham, The Polo Poems,* and several chapbooks. Her fiction includes short stories *Habitats* and a novel *The Diver's Tomb.* She received an NEA Creative Writing Fellowship in 1982 and was named Gilbert-Chappell Distinguished Poet for 2012 and 2013. She served as Hege Professor of Humanities and writer in residence of Guilford College until her retirement in 1992.

Grub

JOSEPHUS III

Author's Note: The Greensboro Grub—People walk in strangers and walk out friends and family, walk in individuals and walk out community. Fifty to sixty gather each month for a meal, for conversation, for a night of sharing and connecting. The most common comment about the Grub is this: "There is no way to tell others about the Grub. They just have to experience it."

We dig in
Fork to plate
Hand to mouth
Heart to heart
And soul to soul
Dig deep to find those things not often seen
Like love
We break bread
Share our lives and our stories across gravy and gravity
Across color lines and religious barriers
Across egos and attitudes

We build
Across from mushrooms that are mellow
3 stories above the elm we blossom
We plant and prosper in fertile soil
South of the tracks we crossover
Create community like rainbows after the storm, we grow
Seasoned smiles line the halls of the arc
Two by two we board
Stairway to heavenly smells
Laughter and light
Dishes dance on tables
Music and miracles
Poetry and percussion
Sit face to face
Eye to eye
Shoulder to shoulder
We boulder our lives
Roll them out for the room to see
Offer a stranger a piece of me
A bedtime story yet to be told
And we all have one

And tonight we become one
A vivid memory of how things could be
Of how things should be
"I pray that tonight you perform a miracle and allow us to love the person sitting across from us more than we love ourselves, Amen"
Because tonight we Grub
Dig in

Poet, mentor, brother, and son JOSEPHUS III is constantly finding ways to break barriers and share his art. Whether teaching in a classroom in Australia, hosting his radio show in Greensboro, or performing on a stage in South Africa, he is an ambassador for the art form, a living reminder that poetry is life and life is poetry.

Home Becoming

TINA FIRESHEETS

I HADN'T INTENDED TO STAY HERE.

I transferred to UNCG my junior year with plans to major in broadcast journalism. But after one meeting with an advisor whose disinterest in my future was pretty clear, I realized I had made a horrible mistake. I should have transferred to UNC-CHAPEL HILL to study print journalism. That was what I really wanted to do. And the student body there actually had school spirit, for God's sake. I was twenty years old, and even though Greensboro had the Four Seasons Mall and Japanese restaurants, I didn't think it was a very exciting place to live.

That, and I totally wasn't prepared for the humidity. I grew up in western North Carolina, where it got hot during the day, but you could count on crisp, cool evenings. You could sit outside under the stars and actually get goosebumps on your arms.

The summer heat in Greensboro made me grumpy and sluggish. My first car was a Chevette. Without air conditioning. It was a relief to get out of it so that I could peel the shirt off my back. My first summer here, I rented an apartment off Spring Garden Street. I shared it with a Chinese international student, who screeched into the phone almost daily with her boyfriend. I could hear her end of their high-pitched conversations through both of our closed bedroom doors. The apartment smelled like nail polish remover, and when I walked into the kitchen, my shoes stuck like gummy tape to the floor. My roommate didn't want to run the air conditioner. My plants died. I woke up feeling nauseous. More signs that I had made a terrible choice in coming to Greensboro. But I didn't feel like I could transfer again. And I had a boyfriend. I also got involved with the campus newspaper.

Then I broke up with the boyfriend and decided to move to California once I graduated. Until I went to college, my mother was the only other Asian person I ever knew. When I received a grant through UNCG to attend a Korean-American students conference in San Francisco, I saw for the first time many people who looked like me. After that experience, I decided I wanted to live there.

But things didn't exactly go as planned. I met a guy I really liked. My mother was diagnosed with lung cancer my senior year, and I just didn't feel right about moving across the country. Eventually I moved in with that guy I really liked. We got married about seven years later, and my mother died a few months afterward.

We remained in Greensboro, setting down roots. I got a job as a reporter for the *News & Record*. When my husband's father was diagnosed with lung cancer, we helped his mother care for him. And when he died, we decided to stay to be near her.

Greensboro has become home for me. People recognize my byline from the newspaper, and my work has given me the opportunity to encounter so many different people. I've interviewed celebrities passing through Greensboro and local shift workers struggling to provide for their families.

I have come to love this city. There are times when I wish it were more than it is, but I defend it like a loyal family member. I can talk smack about Greensboro. But if someone who isn't from here talks smack about it, I get very defensive.

I love Greensboro for its diversity. It's not obvious in the way that it may be in New York or Los Angeles. Greensboro has been resettling refugees since the end of the Vietnam War. Our refugee population includes Vietnamese, Montagnard, Sudanese, Liberian, Bhutanese, Burmese, and Iraqi new arrivals. Their children are our future leaders. More than a hundred first languages are spoken in our public schools.

The best Ethiopian food I've ever eaten was at the home of an Ethiopian refugee down the road in High Point. I wrote a story for the newspaper about an Ethiopian man's reunification with his teenage son. His Eritrean wife cooked a full meal for us. She served us wearing her traditional cultural clothing.

I have written about the Persian New Year tradition, practiced just outside Greensboro, of jumping over a fire. I will never forget the Persian hosts' gracious hospitality and willingness to let me be a part of this special ritual.

I spent an entire day with a Mexican family as they prepared to celebrate their daughter's *quinceañera,* or fifteenth birthday party. They began cooking the *barbacoa,* or beef, at 5 a.m. Nathalie, the young woman celebrating her birthday, was kind, respectful, and appreciative of her parents' efforts. They were a working class family and lived in a modest house. Various family members came to their home to help make salsa or carry things to the event. Nathalie's mother, in particular, seemed tireless that day, never stopping once. She prepared much of the food, helped her daughter through two wardrobe changes, served guests at the party, then helped clear their plates. The affair—complete with a band, photographer, party favors, and full meal—cost as much as some American weddings. Although the family spoke little English, their graciousness needed no translation. I was honored to be a part of that event.

On a personal level, I am glad to live in a city with three Korean restaurants and three Korean hair salons. My Korean hairstylist also cuts my son's hair. I will not force him to go to Korean church or Korean language classes.

But I will let him know that they're available to him, should he choose to pursue them.

Greensboro may be a mid-sized city in the Southeast. Yet, if you ever visit the Greensboro Buddhist Center on Liberty Road, you feel like you've been transported to a corner of Southeast Asia. From the road, the white farmhouse doesn't look out of the ordinary—until you hear the chanting coming from within and see the statues of Buddha outside. It is one of the most peaceful places I've visited in Greensboro. The monks there live simple lives, devoted to Theravada Buddhism. I tried meditating with them one morning. But my mind was too jumpy, my body too undisciplined. It is a place I think of often.

I am no longer trying to leave Greensboro. I've come to accept its idiosyncrasies and appreciate its strengths. I take comfort in its familiarity and find enough change and new development to bring excitement.

I didn't intend to stay.

And yet, that's okay.

TINA FIRESHEETS is a writer and editor of *1808: Greensboro's Magazine.* She was a reporter for the *News & Record* for almost fifteen years. Her many beats included education, retail, and general assignment; but her most rewarding years were those she spent as a feature writer.

Street Scenes

Greensboro Beautiful

STUART DISCHELL

I AM NOT THE TYPE OF WRITER who knows the names of flowers and trees; nevertheless, I enjoy walking among them nearly every day in the Greensboro Arboretum. A born-again pagan, I like to witness sunrise and sunset, especially on the solstices and equinoxes. Jeff the Dog has accompanied me almost every day of his life. He must understand Latin because when I say the word *arboretum,* he cocks his head and has an intelligent demeanor. His interest in greenery is much more than any human's, and he is at home here, wearing down his nails on the concrete path. Pulling toward the lawns and beds, he has his own sets of rituals.

When the arboretum is astonishingly empty of people, I can hear the crows fussing with a hawk or see the snake that lives in North Buffalo Creek or the blue heron that leaves its footprints in the mud. Some mornings I bump into my friend the folksinger and we stop and wag our chins about traveling and kids and writing and music-making and every topic under the sun. I have known him for as many as the twenty-some years I have lived in Greensboro. He has performed his songs all over the country and was a good enough sport to entertain at my daughter's birthday parties when she was little. Jeff has learned it's best to sit when Bruce and I talk because it's often for a good long time.

Although I have exchanged introductions with a few of my fellow dog-walkers, I mostly recall the names of their animals—Duffy, Miss Ella Fitzgerald, Raya Sunshine, Simon, Moose, Kiya, Gretta, Millie, Pepper, Biscuit, Samson, and Mr. Ollie. I am not the only one with a human-recollection deficit. Just the other day, a patron in a restaurant said to me, "You're Jeff's owner, aren't you?" As if a person could *own* a dog like Jeff. In this manner, a canine has given me my most precious identity in Greensboro. I am not known as Caroline or Adam's dad or Professor Dischell, certainly not the broken-hearted, sensitive poet. I am the guy with the Red Sox cap who walks the big, crazy dog.

Greensboro is a provincial city in the best sense. People say hello to each other on the streets, it's easy to find a parking space, and the cost of living is relatively low. Keeping pace with globalization, its stores and restaurants have undergone huge changes over the years. It's possible now to consume the produce and cheeses, wines and legumes and coffees of the world. In nearby Lindley Park, at "the corner," the Bestway—once a funky, run-down neighborhood supermarket—has been transformed by its current owners into a cool place to buy vegetables and fish. It hosts the Wall of Beer, one of the largest selections of domestic and global brews in the Southeast.

Originally part of the vast J. Van Lindley Tree Nursery, the arboretum was created in the early nineties by a partnership between the city and Greensboro Beautiful, an organization that has also crafted several other lovely parks. Make no mistake, I am not saying Greensboro is the Paris of the South. No electrical towers or power lines grace the Jardin du Luxembourg. In the Greensboro Arboretum there are no carrousels, pony rides, puppet shows, or a café to have coffee and pastry under the trees. At times it's hard to lose oneself in one's thoughts here when cop cars and ambulances race by on adjacent Wendover Avenue. Still, the arboretum has its sculptures and gorgeous seasonal beds of local and international plantings. Sadly, Jeff would not be permitted in the Jardin du Luxembourg.

Sometimes I imagine illicit lovers meet in the parking lots of the arboretum and the nearby recreation areas. Otherwise, not much drama takes place, except on the nearby baseball fields during Little League games. On occasion, fellow dog-walkers break down their anonymity and discuss more than their pets. Besides the array of older neighbors and Greensboro locals, some of the people I greet are a Scottish photographer of the blues, an artisan cabinetmaker from Connecticut, an insurance executive from New York state, a restaurant manager from Mexico, a retired editor from Wales, an organic weaver from Minnesota, the extremely dedicated and friendly park workers, dozens of familiar runners, and strolling families who are the newest North Carolinians—immigrants from all over the globe. This gives me hope that one day I, too, might fit in.

Some mornings I compose poems in my head when I am walking in the arboretum. This one evolved over the course of a few weeks, and I tried not to write it down until it was finished.

A Different Kind of Person

I encounter a woman from a long way off
Almost every morning when I walk my dog
In a certain park between certain hours
That have not changed the whole season long.
She owns several coats, all of them
The same length, yesterday a gray one;
Today deep red, and she smoothed her
Cheek as she went by. She sees me
At my worst, unshaven, in my sweats,
Bagging dog shit, my son's skateboard cap

Pulled down to my eyebrows. Hers arch
When she says "Good morning" which is all
I have ever heard her speak with her accent
From somewhere between the Danube
And the Don, where I bet she modeled coats
In a capital city. How she got here or what
She does is none of my business, and I
Do not wish to say to her more than, "Good
Morning," or ask, "How are you today?"
And spoil the peace we have found among
The ornamental trees native to our region.

STUART DISCHELL is the author of several books, including *Evenings & Avenues, Dig Safe,* and *Backwards Days.* His poems have been published in the *Atlantic,* the *New Republic, Slate, Kenyon Review,* and other publications. A recipient of awards from the National Endowment for the Arts, North Carolina Arts Council, and John Simon Guggenheim Foundation, he is a professor in the MFA program in creative writing at the University of North Carolina at Greensboro.

Cake Haven

KATIE SAINTSING

I WAS RAISED IN THE KIND of leafy-green neighborhood for which Greensboro is famous.

But I *grew up* behind a bakery counter in a strip mall on one of the city's busiest thoroughfares.

The bakery, Maxie B's, was where I started to figure out what it actually means to be an adult—that is, beyond taking home a paycheck and feeling free to eat a second piece of cake.

The job was my first, and I was eager to please. I already had a special connection to the bakery: Years before, my family had a Friday night ritual that included dinner at Lox Stock & Bagel—a Greensboro institution— followed by a visit to the video store around the corner, where my brothers and I had to agree on one movie.

Then dessert. A couple of doors down from the video store was I Can't Believe It's Yogurt. The place was nothing fancy: standard-issue franchise décor, with a green-and-white-tiled floor and a backlit menu with pic- tures above the counter. On the counter where we sat and ate, there were always small vases with flowers. During the week, we were an eat-dinner-on-the-fly kind of family, but come Friday, we were all a little more relaxed, and that one small detail made us feel welcome to sit awhile and enjoy our dessert.

I'm not sure when or why we stopped spending those Friday nights together—life got busier, more complicated—but at some point when we weren't paying attention, the yogurt shop transformed into a bakery called Maxie B's. The frozen yogurt and ice cream were still on the menu, but cakes and cookies and cupcakes had been added, too. By the time I started working there, customers crossed a patio lined with fairy lights to enter a store with hardwood floors, a beadboard counter with a tin backsplash, chairs with cushions, and a fake fireplace that emitted real heat. A new generation of families—and couples on dates and friends catching up— lingered around tables like my family used to do.

Every detail of the store was perfect. And that made me want to be a little more perfect, too.

The work wasn't always easy. There were nights when I was pretty sure all of Greensboro was lined up in front of me: grandmas with grandkids, businesspeople still in their suits, gaggles of high schoolers.

They all seemed to come at once, and for hours during some shifts, there was nothing my coworkers and I could do except focus on helping one person at a time, refilling yogurt machines and cupcake trays and stacks of cups when they got low.

They stood in front of the ice cream case, the cupcake case, snaked around the tables and out the door. They didn't seem to mind the waiting. They leaned in to look through the glass at tubs of cookies 'n cream, butter pecan, moose tracks, and cappuccino crunch. They cooed over trays of red velvet cupcakes, Oreo buttercream cupcakes, chocolate cupcakes with cream cheese icing. They paced around and around cake stands display- ing devil's food, pumpkin chocolate chip, strawberry buttercream, steeling themselves for what must have been the most important decision in their lives at that moment.

I understand that now: After a long day of making decisions of varying degrees of importance, it's a relief to get exactly the thing you want, with no regrets.

There are always rough patches in customer service jobs. You're on your feet for many hours, and people can be gruff. But it was hard to be unhappy in such a bright, sweet place. Cake and ice cream make people happy, and it was fun to field a question—"What's a brownstone front cake?" "What's a hummingbird cake?"—even if it was the hundredth time, if the answer got an excited reaction.

Outside the shop, my life was more chaotic: I was involved in too many extracurriculars and overwhelmed by schoolwork and nervous about applying to college and too concerned with my friends, and I got upset on a daily basis, it seemed, with something or someone at home. It's easy to forget now how hard it is to be a teenager, but at the time, for me, Maxie B's was an oasis of calm. It felt good to go somewhere with a routine, a to-do list, and consistent beginning and ending times. When the rush subsided every evening, there was the satisfying work of closing the place down—the small pleasures of making sure a freshly washed plastic cake dome dried with no water spots, taking a scrub brush to drip trays, putting everything in its place for the start of a new day. Often I left the store covered in a thin, sticky film of sugar and dairy product, and smelling like frozen yogurt. Sometimes I'd reach into my pockets the next day and find cake crumbs. Yet it felt good to be all in, to make sure every detail was just right, to be part of creating an experience. I went home tired, but in the best possible way.

This idea of individual experiences, of attending to details that would mean the most to other people, became central to every shift I worked. I discovered that when it came to the long lines, there was no point in getting frantic. The only thing to do was to treat every person like he or she were the only customer in line. Everyone deserved a little conversation with their cake and coffee, and those conversations sustained me, too.

That seems obvious now, but to an otherwise self-absorbed teenager, it was a revelation: I could come to work, and the outside world—the unfinished college application, the tough day at school, the fight with my mom—didn't matter, because it wasn't about me.

It was about the mom with a toddler on her hip or the elderly couple or that one girl who always talked a little too loud. It was about the regular customers: the lawyer who'd been coming to the shop for so long that he still ordered the off-the-menu yogurt pies that were a staple of the old franchise—and who astonished me years later by walking into the Chapel Hill yogurt shop where I worked in college. Or, the man who so predictably ordered vanilla yogurt with maple walnuts halfway up that I started getting his order ready as soon as I saw him. The woman who always ordered some combination of large, low-fat, low-sugar flavors when she came in nearly every night close to closing time so she could chat with us—and who fixed small gift bags for those of us who went off to college the next fall. For her, I think, those visits were never as much about the yogurt as they were about seeing friendly faces.

Not long after I started working at Maxie B's, I showed up for my shift to find out that my coworker had been in a fender bender and wouldn't be coming in. A replacement was coming, but she'd be late.

For an hour, I raced around behind the counter while the store filled with people. It wasn't long before the line wound through the store and out the door.

"Are you by yourself back there?" customers said. "Looks like you could use some help."

One woman told me she wished she could throw on some work clothes and help me out.

I'm not sure I realized at the time how lucky I was. In another time, in another place, people might have gotten annoyed. They might have grown antsy and jostled in line. They might have been rude to me or made a big point of leaving.

But that night in the Gate City, the people of Greensboro did what they could for me: They recognized that I was just a kid, in the midst of growing up, learning to do a job, and they showed me kindness and patience. And when everyone in line had been helped, they actually broke into applause. I'm sure I blushed, but the truth is, I've never forgotten that shift.

It's an odd sensation to go back to the scene of an old job, a place that was once so much a part of my life, where I'd had such a strong sense of purpose. The trivial tasks, the ones I used to do every day—counting down a register, cleaning a yogurt machine—aren't familiar to me anymore. I can go to Maxie B's and marvel over how the shop has expanded, notice the special touches in every corner, sit and linger over coffee and catch up with a friend. There's no evidence of my ever having been there—constant change is the way of such places. But when I look at the girl behind the counter, the one who's trying hard, who's probably dealing with the pressures of home and school and work, who's still in the process of becoming who she'll one day be, I recognize myself. I was once that girl. And I know she'll be okay, if she lets the job teach her patience and kindness and pride in the details. Part of growing up is learning that hard work can make life sweet.

After refining her sweet tooth at Maxie B's, **KATIE SAINTSING** graduated from the University of North Carolina at Chapel Hill and returned to Greensboro. Today, she gets to know her fellow North Carolinians not behind a counter, but behind a reporter's notebook as a writer and editor at *Our State* magazine.

What-A-Burger

The Hamburger of the Gate City

JERI ROWE

EVERY TIME I GO, I almost miss it.

It comes up quick just beyond a loping curve near the skating rink. The faint smell of grilling hamburgers hovers like a cloud over the parking lot of gravel and dirt, and it sits so close to North Church Street you can hear the whoosh of traffic through the big window.

No matter. The place reminds me of baseball, summer, and honeysuckle on a vine, and when I walk in and hear the jingle of a single bell above the door, the same thought hits me every time.

Nothing has changed.

The red-checked curtains.

The eight stools, six tables, and four booths.

The one Elvis clock on the wall above a poem written by a longtime customer named Bud. He calls it "To say Thank You."

Yep, same old place. Same old tiny place.

When I mention Church Street Drive-In to anyone, they look puzzled. But mention What-A-Burger, they get it then. Everyone knows it by *that* name.

Sure, the name *What-A-Burger* is painted big on the side of the building. And sure, you see its creation painted big on the wall—a circle of ground beef made with mayonnaise, lettuce, tomato, sliced onions, and a pickle on a hamburger bun.

But it's the history that makes this place.

Ask a Page High grad or anyone who remembers the mill whistle. What-A-Burger has anchored two spots within a four-block radius on North Church Street since 1959, and for many, it has become *the* hamburger of the Gate City.

What-A-Burger has fed generations of Page students. It is remembered too as the place that once cashed the checks of thousands of textile workers who worked in mills with names as familiar as church to so many: White Oak, Revolution, and Proximity.

It must've been quite the sight back then. On Thursday nights every payday, mill workers would get in line to have their checks cashed, and that line would wrap around the building like a cat's tail. Everyone who came wanted the same thing: their money and a burger.

But here's what gets me: Other than a four-year hiatus three decades ago, the place has been run by the same family.

And they're still there.

Kathy Beaman manages the place. She calls it a "café." At age four, she started there stacking bottles. She's now in her sixties and wears a white mechanic's shirt adorned with two patches, *Church Street Drive-In* and *Kathy.* Her *Kathy* patch is over her heart.

Her two teenage grandsons, Austin Laws and Brenden Pegram, wash dishes, take orders, and clean. Her teenage granddaughter, Raine Pegram, takes drink orders.

Meanwhile, her surrogate son, Rick Jones, mans the grills and makes at least one hundred and fifty What-A-Burgers a day. He grew up eating them. He's now in his mid-thirties, and every day at work he sits in front of the grill wearing a blue shirt bearing the patch *Lil Rick.*

His dad, see, is Rick—Slick to his friends.

The picture of Kathy's daughter, Trisha Ann Laws, sits on a shelf behind the counter above the security-camera TV in front of a set of ceramic frogs. I ask. Kathy answers.

"She used to work here," Kathy says.

Then, she tells me the rest of the story.

That includes one of the last things her daughter ever said to her: "Mama, please raise my children for me. I don't want no one else to have 'em."

When she told her mother that, Trisha Ann was twenty-seven, a single mother of four children. She was lying in a hospital bed at Cone Health diagnosed with something I can barely spell, let alone understand.

Wegener's granulomatosis.

Kathy tells me it's a rare vascular lung disease. My cyberspace research tells me it's a rare autoimmune disorder. Whatever it is, I do know this: One month Trisha Ann was fine, cleaning hotel rooms and waiting tables at Church Street Drive-In. The next month, she was scrambling to stay alive. Kathy stayed by her bedside, telling her to hold on.

"You don't have to worry, Baby, don't you worry about it," Kathy told her. "You'll be home, taking care of them, too."

That didn't happen. Several days later, Trisha Ann died. When she did, Kathy's head lay on her daughter's shoulder. She was praying. "God, please take care of her. You gave her to me for a little while. Now, I have to give her back to you."

In the photo above the security-camera TV, Trisha Ann looks no more than fifteen with brown hair trailing way past her shoulders and wearing a Mickey Mouse T-shirt that looks way too big. Her photo is tucked into a frame that reads, *Remember the Good Times*.

I ask Kathy how she broke the news to her grandchildren.

"I looked at their little faces and said, 'God has taken your Momma home,'" she says. "Austin (the oldest) jumped up and ran outside. It broke my heart so bad. The other three, well, Brenden, he was six and he knew what I was talking about, and I told him, 'No, your Mom is not coming home.' But Caleb, he was four and Raine was not quite two. They had no idea."

That was more than a decade ago. Since then, Kathy has kept her promise. She has raised Trisha Ann's children like they were her own. See, Trisha Ann never married Austin's dad because she fell in love with the dad of the other three children.

So, everything fell on Kathy.

As I listen, I ask more questions. Kathy tells me about the tradition on Mother's Day and on October 27, Trisha Ann's birthday. They all go to Greensboro's Lakeview Memorial Cemetery off U.S. 29 to pay respects. Kathy tells me how Trisha Ann's children go to her grave, one by one, and release balloons. Their mom loved balloons. She tells me all but Caleb work at What-A-Burger. She tells me the cute photo by the ceramic frogs is a picture of Austin as a kindergartner.

Then, she tells me why her daughter's photo will always be there.

"She existed. To remind everybody. She shouldn't be forgotten."

I hear all that from my perch at the bottom of the counter near the big TV.

As more stories come, I realize What-A-Burger is as much a part of Greensboro as the big-time ACC men's basketball tournament at the coliseum off East Lee and the annual major-league golf tournament that started at Sedgefield Country Club in 1938.

Both events are full of tradition. What-A-Burger is, too.

It reminds me of the old Boar & Castle restaurant, the legendary teen hangout just west of downtown. Locals loved that place. They have stories they tell their grandchildren, and they have stories they only tell their friends.

Yeah, Boar & Castle could be a rambunctious, randy kind of place. But Boar & Castle closed decades ago. Church Street Drive-In — excuse me, What-A-Burger — remains. And like Boar & Castle once did, What-A-Burger remains the wallpaper of the lives of the young, the working class, and the long-timers who still call Greensboro home.

Long-timers, like Fran Truitt. That's Kathy's mom. She started What-A-Burger in 1959. She and her first husband opened the first Church Street

Drive-In where the Kangaroo service station now sits four blocks north. She was the cook, the carhop, the waitress. She started her restaurant career in Greensboro at age twenty-two, when she was pregnant with her last child, her fifth.

She's now in her late seventies, with a new right hip and her almost new right hand. A year ago, she had surgery to help her deal with what she calls "RA," rheumatoid arthritis. The cast on her hand was all wires and rubber bands, a scary-looking contraption that reminds her daughter of the film, *A Nightmare on Elm Street.*

"That looks like something Freddy Krueger would wear," Kathy likes to say.

When I find Fran, she has yet to come back to work. She's sitting at the end of the counter beside the big TV. She's watching TV Land, first *The Andy Griffith Show,* then *Gunsmoke.*

Like those shows, she is a classic. Everyone knows her. She's Fran to many, Mama Fran to some, and Francis to Bud, the poet of the poem pasted to the wall beneath the Elvis clock. On the back of Church Street Drive-In's menu is a personal message Fran has written for every customer to read: *Thank you for your business, Fran Truitt (owner).*

Fran knows so many customers by face, by name, by their order, and by how they've grown up—from high school, to college, from first job, to fourth, to all the responsibilities and heartaches that come along the way.

"I've seen people from going to school, to getting engaged, to getting married, to having babies, to getting grandbabies, and I always wonder where the time went," she tells me. "I ain't got no older."

I laugh. But I laugh a lot in front of Lil Rick's grill.

I hear the banter from their customers. Kathy calls them "nuts." It goes on all day long. I hear about how customers hold up one finger or two. Kathy knows exactly what they want. Or they simply walk in. Like Clarence "Pop" Tart. He's been coming for a half century and getting the same thing: What-A-Burger with no pickle, half order of french fries, and a tea.

I hear about the Elvis clock, a gift from a customer. Then, I hear about the why: Fran is a big Elvis Presley fan, and she caught his scarf during his show at the Greensboro Coliseum. You know that show was a long time ago. Anyway, someone offered her $500 to give it up. She said no. She still has it.

Then, I hear about the car. Or really, the Jeep Grand Cherokee.

It was May 4, 2013, a Saturday, a few minutes before 5 a.m. Kathy was awakened by a ringing phone. It was her brother Ricky, the jokester. He told her a car was in the café.

"Don't call and wake me up!" she told him. "If there is not a car in that building, your head will be in that building!"

She drove up there and saw a ring of fire trucks and police cars—and a dark gray Grand Cherokee whose entire front end was inside the restaurant. The SUV, with a seventeen-year-old driver, had careened off North Church, crossed Denny Road, and hit the restaurant's basement wall, two inches from a gas line.

"If he had hit that," a firefighter told Kathy, "there would be a hole in the ground" where the restaurant had once stood.

The driver was uninjured. He was lucky. The café wasn't.

For nearly five months, Church Street Drive-In remained closed. Kathy worried, saved, and scrimped. Raising her daughter's four children, who ranged in ages from twelve to nineteen at that time, she was left with no income. But when it got tough, she received an unannounced cash gift from a member at her church, Lake Brandt Baptist.

Fran worried, too. She spent $30,000 of her own money to repair the damage not covered by insurance. Like Kathy, she had no money coming in either. She knew she'd reopen. The restaurant had never been closed in its history for that long. Still, the money she spent hit her hard.

Then, she listened to the radio and heard all these people talking about her restaurant and talking about her. Kathy ran into people at the grocery store. She ended up staying two hours, telling people about the accident and their future.

Both mother and daughter knew that they had to reopen. They did finally on September 23, 2013. It was a Monday.

"Oh my, we were so busy," Fran says from her perch beside the TV. "It was like old times. But since then, it's backed off. I think it's the economy. So many of our customers who go to work have come in and said, 'This is my last day.' They told me while I was cooking, and I think, 'Lord, what's going on?'

"It was a lot of them, not just one or two. Jobs ain't easy to find. You get one, you'd better keep it."

Andy Griffith becomes Matt Dillon, and Fran stops to talk to yet another customer.

I get up from my stool in front of Lil Rick's grill to read the poem on the wall beneath the Elvis clock, the one that Jasper "Bud" Brady wrote for Fran fifteen years ago. His last few lines are these:

> I hope you stay open, at least a hundred years.
> As long as you're on Church Street,
> there'll be smiles instead of tears.

People will always believe that. And it's not just Pop Tart and Bud.

JERI ROWE worked for nearly a quarter century for the *News & Record*. At his last assignment there, he spent eight years as the newspaper's staff columnist. And yes, he has eaten at What-A-Burger more than once.

Sense of Place

A Short Story

STEVE MITCHELL

I OPEN MY EYES, not quite knowing where I am. Knowing the car, knowing the wheels beneath me. Opening my eyes to the road, to a dark and foreign road unfolding before me. The hiss of the tires, the featureless night. I open my eyes just enough to place myself. In the car beside Caleb.

The car is thick with sleep. And the heat rising from the pink, spindly limbs of the girls, snoring softly in the back seat. Suits still damp, sandals still sandy. All of us sun-baked, hot-skinned and drowsy, our clothes pricking us in tender places.

It has its own uncertain poetry: the night, the car, the road. A blurred and formless comfort. Something anticipatory, not yet accepted; a question asked yet left unanswered, not abandoned but held in pause.

Caleb has turned the radio on low and rolled down his window, which means he's getting sleepy. A late-night breeze spins through the car. I should keep him company but I don't want to sit up in the seat. I don't want talk. I want to drift where I am, loose and liminal, riding the unseen waves of the road.

Earlier in the evening, Abby and Meghan had recounted the trip to each other in the back seat. Meghan taking the lead, then Abby joining in with her older sister: the way the sand squished between their toes when a wave slid in, the dolphins we'd spotted from the balcony, the holes dug and castles built, the surfers. They traded memories back and forth. Occasionally, they'd draw me in. Remember that, Momma? Do you remember?

Later, Meghan read to Abby, she in her seatbelt, Abby in her car seat. She tilted the picture books in Abby's direction, page by page, and plucked another from the stack in the seat. Then, just before sleep, they began to whisper, voices low and giggly, the pauses between them sometimes so long it was impossible to tell whether they were speaking from dream. The landscape beneath the road shifted from the still surface of sand to gentle curves and swells. The sun dropped beyond the trees and we fell asleep, leaving Caleb to navigate us, through tiny towns on two-lane highways, back to our lives.

Eyes closed, there is only motion and the slight sway of the breeze. Eyes closed, everything in me slows and settles into my breath. My breathing steady, it's a sense of place I feel. Or of being placed.

Caleb sighs and the car begins to slow, coming to a halt, and I know we're at the singular stoplight of a small town. There's something familiar in the thrilled stillness of the night. The pause. Caleb releases a slow breath. I hear the stoplight click to red above us.

Alex is standing in the intersection under the light at Washington and Elm. I'm on the sidewalk. It's four in the morning, maybe five. I'm twenty or twenty-one. Alex raises his arms in a ridiculous hieratic gesture and lets out a slow, sensual moan.

We'd seen a band at the Blind Tiger. I can't remember the band, only that the music had been loud, slow, complex, building to great washes which broke over our heads and that Alex had closed his eyes for most of the show, swaying in his hips, arms loose at his sides, and I stood awkwardly beside him, trying to find my place, trying to find a way to enjoy what I knew I was enjoying, trying to voice that joy in my body.

"My God. My God! Can you believe what we just heard?" he'd shouted in the parking lot, his body still jointless, spasming from the music. "Man, I can't go home now," he declared. "I need to walk. Will you walk with me?"

I'd call this memory but it's not really that at all. It's simply a part of me, something vital threaded through sinew and bone. It opens all at once and I'm captured in its fine strands, in the way I'm often stolen away by something behind me. I'll lose the now altogether to some shadow, not completely the present while not exactly the past, the real trick of the past being that it isn't the past at all; I bring every moment of it forward with me.

We'd had a lot to drink earlier, Alex and I, but that is wearing away now, leaving a quiet softness in its wake. Somehow, without making the decision, we walk away from the bars and the ragged noise of campus, toward downtown. There are tree-lined residential streets and blocks of warehouses or empty buildings. It had rained while we were in the club. The road glistens, all the colors of the night a little smeared. The trees drip, a random droplet plunking our shoulder or splattering in our hair. The only sound is an occasional passing car sliding by us with a hiss.

We walk and talk. About anything. Everything. At first, it's Alex, in great surges of words, sentences muscling forward, jumping track, colliding with others. He talks in a rush of excitement, beginning with the night and the music, but sweeping everything in his path, as if attempting to house all the world within his sentences. Gradually this enthusiasm infects me, or wears at my defenses, until I match his exaltations with my own.

He tells me about an eighth-grade teacher who acknowledged him, captured him, nurtured him. About a school field trip to a museum a few years later where he'd found one painting so completely alive he wanted to remain before it for hours. He tells me about the new *Godspeed You! Black Emperor* album, the earthy, resonant churn of the music.

"It's like a kind of message from another world," he tells me. "And I don't have to understand it, 'cause I know it already."

I drift in the gap between my guarded self and the certainty of my own joys. I'd moved from the hinterlands to the big city for college and, in my second year, having thawed from my freshman awe, I desperately want to be somebody, anybody, other than who I am. Yet it's strangely liberating, drafting in Alex's ecstasy, to tell him of my own. My sentences begin in a familiar place but veer into the unexpected, or the ground drops beneath them, and I find myself scrambling for something higher or more solid.

We walk and walk. We talk. I tell him things about myself I don't know; at least, not until they are said. There are no tragic or shameful secrets. Instead, we find a vocabulary of wonder to share. Something birthed in the gravity of the music. Some call answered between us, taken up between us. Without thought, without thinking.

I tell him about standing beneath a bracing waterfall, the icy water battering me until my body was made of mist and spray. Of watching my grandmother cook a meal, her wide hands mixing biscuits, her fingers tender with the dough as she dropped soft clumps to the metal sheet. The way her meals warmed and soothed me. I tell him about hearing Patti Smith's *Horses* for the first time.

We're tired. Our bodies steamed in the heat of the club and the press of others against us, our limbs weak from standing, swaying in the buffeting force of the music. It's very late or very early and we walk though our calves ache and we are thirsty, walking because we're caught in this communion, something strange and unexpected yet embraced completely.

There are silences also, deep silences that the hush of the night only deepens. And for a moment it seems every word shared has made this vibrant silence possible. We've lured each other into stillness.

When we turn the corner from Market to Elm, Alex's eyes glitter. "This way," he says, "I want to see trains."

The sidewalk shines in the rain. The street is black, still water, an occasional splash of neon rippling its surface. The storefronts are dark or dimly lit, a hollow, abandoned space next door to an inviting store hung with bright dresses, lined with rainbow rows of shoes. The store aisles are vacant, the restaurant tables empty. We've emptied ourselves with our words; now every nerve ending sparks and dances. The night around us is nearly painful. The fact of a city street, the fact of another human being, it's overwhelming.

We stand at the tracks, peering down the carved path of the rails in both directions, first one, then the other. We wait, side by side. And we are quiet then, a pleasant exhaustion rising in us, giving our body weight again where the words before had made us light. We wait patiently for one train, then another; the first a short passenger, its windows revealing sleepy or sleeping faces; the second an enormous freight train, cars rocking by us in all colors and shapes. When the last car is out of sight and the rails no longer tremble, we turn back up Elm.

At the corner of Washington and Elm, I realize Alex is no longer at my side. He's standing in the center of the intersection, his arms raised to the night sky. The stoplight clicks to red. He lets out this low, sensual moan, something sated and tremulous. I feel his moan in my body, outward into my fingers and toes, and I can't help but smile, then laugh. He cocks his head toward me, a crooked grin playing on his face. And his face is so open and guileless, his eyes so clear, he's so completely himself before me, that there is no response but love.

I can't help but love him and love him completely. I imagine this is the instant painters anticipate before their subjects, waiting patiently for the flash when masks fall away to reveal a true face.

It's the moment Abby sees the ocean for the first time, coming to a full stop as she crests the dune. She doesn't know she's motionless. She thinks she's still running, but she's completely still for an instant before she raises her arms above her head, shouting something—not words, something before words or above words—then running to the surf just to her ankles, squealing and dancing back. It's something more than love.

It's the incidental, shattering glance with a stranger on the street, the moment our eyes accidentally meet and we haven't had a chance to hide.

Open and unguarded, we see into each other for an instant. And we know each other, all at once. A shock of recognition. It's nothing but adoration. A form of worship.

I want to hold the moment of seeing forever. I want to study Alex's face the way I might kneel before a beautiful painting, the way I might grow completely stilled in the face of music. I want to take it into myself in gasps as I might a mountaintop view or an open sunrise.

The blue night is easing toward morning. The flat, empty lanes extend in each direction. I can see the indigo sky and ridges of cloud in the corridor between buildings. The stoplight clicks to green, and Alex extends his hand, his palm upturned and open. I step down from the sidewalk.

We've been shedding skins, all evening, with each step, with every word. And though we'll certainly slip back into them again, tonight they've been sloughing off, and now we hold each other, empty and naked as the light changes above us.

It's something like praise. Whisper choruses sounding behind me, insinuating themselves when I least expect, whispers of occasional comforts and graces reminding me what is true. A thankfulness I feel watching Abby tiptoe forward into the lapping waves, arms pin-wheeling, then reel back, breathless.

Dancing with Alex beneath the stoplight like something from a Fred Astaire movie, right hands clasped and held aloft, left at our waists, dancing to a melody we're inventing or remembering, one eye on the street for traffic, our bodies don't feel like bodies at all, but like an alien music bound to earth only by our breath, like a huge, spreading flower swaying on the spindle of a stem.

A lone early morning runner jogs up Elm. Seeing us, he spins, still jogging, a full turn, applauding silently before continuing on.

I love Alex because I see him, see him clearly, perfectly, for an instant. And, having seen him, how can I not love him. How can this seeing not shake me, not take my breath, leave a soft scar of intimacy. It's strong, rampant, directionless. How can there ever be too much love in the world.

That night, at the corner of Washington and Elm, it's a place he inhabits in me. As if love isn't a feeling but a location as physical as the street itself. A location that can only be shared. A place to stand.

The adoration I feel listening to my daughters sleep, the warm scent of their skin and hair. It comes over me without cause, in the passing contact with a stranger on the street or the sudden presence of Alex or the private whispers of a couple at the next table, as a swell and a catch in the throat. All the words I used with Alex that night to try to define my place within the burn and sway of the world, all the words that tumbled out of me, undisguised. It's something I claimed, for the first time, that night.

I open my eyes. Caleb's features are soft in the glow of the dashboard lights. Gray trees spin by the window and the waves of the road are more pronounced now, gradual hills rising and falling. His hair is tossed by the breeze and he needs a shave. He's humming softly to a tune on the radio, fingers spidering along the top of the steering wheel, humming the way he did in the moments after Meghan's birth.

He stands by the bed, Meghan bundled in his arms, her eyes wide before him. He sways with her side to side. Before the birth, his terror with the thought of a child had been palpable, leaking through as a tightness in his voice, a panicked glance. But in this moment, this first moment, he vanishes into her. As if her gaze takes him in so completely that he disappears for an instant, his expression silent and awed. I can see the room around him has faded; even I have faded for a moment. It's just he and Meghan locked into something so powerful that he loses all thought and all pretense. He's absolutely beautiful.

In a moment he begins to sway gently, side to side, while the nurse busies herself with my pulse and the CNA gathers the bedding, and I let my head fall back for an instant to the pillow. He begins to sing, to hum to her. A spontaneous tune. He doesn't know he's singing; he doesn't even know he's breathing.

So many private things pass between them. A language is there I cannot enter. In that instant they know each other absolutely. It's a wordless and constant knowing, completely their own. It is impossible. How can there ever be too much love in the world.

Abby is muttering in her sleep, thick liquid sentences. Or perhaps she's sharing a story with Meghan, her head slumped left in the car seat, her hands folded in her lap. Meghan rustles, shifting position, licking her lips.

One day I'll tell Caleb about Alex. I'll find the words to share this tenderness with him. I don't doubt he'll understand. I imagine the curious spark in his eye, a curl of a smile as he listens. But not tonight, with the glow upon me; not tonight, my skin tingling with Alex's touch. Tonight there are no words.

I open my eyes. Knowing the car, knowing the wheels beneath me. Opening my eyes to a dark and foreign road before me. The hiss of the tires, the featureless night. I open my eyes to place myself. In the car beside Caleb.

"Hey there," he says, noticing me stir. "What's up?"

I stifle a yawn. "Nothing," I say. I wind away from the seat, uncurling, pressing my bare toes into the floor of the car until my legs are fully extended.

Caleb arches an eyebrow in mock surprise. "Nothing?"

I take his hand from where it's dropped to his thigh, twining my fingers into his. "Not a thing."

He glances over and smiles. I rub my eyes with my loose hand, turning in the seat, my back to the door to study his face. In the glow of the dashboard lights with the gray trees streaking by the window.

The smile has settled into his face. I can feel it trickle into his fingers. He glances over again. We'll be home soon.

STEVE MITCHELL's work has been published in numerous publications, including the *Southeast Review*, *storySouth*, the *North Carolina Literary Review*, and *Contrary*. His short story collection, *The Naming of Ghosts*, is published by Press 53. He thinks of self as a verb, believing that writing and reading capture the self in motion. He's co-owner of Scuppernong Books in Greensboro.

Greensboro, A Poem in Prose

VERÓNICA GROSSI

CICADAS, HANGING FROM ABOVE OR BELOW, at the root of oaks and tulip poplars weave a canopy of swirling sizzles. Suspended in the air, the languishing leaves fall onto my window. Between my eyes and the world, the greenery. I hear nothing. A frantic rasp undulates. From another window, a tall sunflower bowing, exhausted from loneliness and no response from above, had sought the rays of the sun looking at its face daringly, opening its big pointy leaves to the sides, in a morning dance, poised with grace, breathing air, quenching its thirst on prickly sun sparkles. Now it looks down sad and exhausted. Its multiple eyes or mouths, silvery seeds with delicate etchings are still buried in its brown skin. When will they fall? First the squirrels will jump at its neck to topple its head and gnaw at it furiously. Now the birds upside down poke at its seeds one by one with sharp precision. The blue-grayish ivy creeps silently, suffocating slowly the orange dapples on fire of marigolds, leaving in the shade other green geometries.

How many layers of veil keep me away from the dangling carousel, the train going in circles? Rolling waves of metallic sound. Nowhere I can imagine the familiar barking of dogs. I cannot hear them. They are numbed in my ears. There is cotton, gray cotton in the air. My eyes cannot penetrate the colors of flowers. They are coagulated vowels, paralyzed dances. The bees fly on a blanket dim and ignored. The tomatoes grow into insipid pinks, wounded on the sides, uneven, hanging sadly, abandoned. Where have the bees gone? The summer is not over yet there is even more silence over the invisible life. Newly opened roses give themselves sideways for no reason, casting their heads in an embarrassing bright red. My house is not still. It drifts on a humid tapestry. How can I rest and find comfort? There is no image, lullaby, or caress in a mysterious suspended corner where traveling has no end. What load do they carry up and down the air? Every night I hear it, the sound of chains, the laments, the muffled sighs and voices, the hidden bodies under the roots of trees, moaning, sobbing, silenced, exhausted from work, wounded by lashes, humiliated.

190

The echoes of games in a floating stadium. No faces, only distant screams and fireworks. I can never see. I never saw a soul walking narrow corridors. Downtown, a whole family crosses the street like a river on tip-toes and colorful shirts, lollipops, sunglasses. What are they looking for? What are they? Superimposed images on a surface whose shape I cannot recognize and forget the next moment, after a wave of light and heat obliterates me further. All I can grab is a silent trail of pain oozing from the pavement, breaking into needles of reflections, hiding again in the corners, flowing with the traffic, the heavy cars that make no difference, that stop at the red light, and make no difference. They could be there or not. Why are they cruising at midday? It is hard to cross such a river of people and voices, once there, kept outside, and away, now whimpering, forever, deep under, without the shade of trees, perhaps without water, much further down in the underground, beneath the foul smell of an obese castaway standing unnoticed, asking for money, with all his drawings in front of a consignment store of shoes too big for anybody, once owned by a rich white woman, now old, sick, and abandoned at a nursing home, smelling of mold and staleness.

The glass offers me the infinite shapes of leaves hanging in movement, each swaying delicately every second differently, in solitude under the gray veil of the day. Nothing seems home. I dig my hands in the soil searching for smells. The worms are wet and hide away. I wait but no one comes. Where are the crowds in the long street downtown that used to house stores with a tram that went up and down? The heart of the road is made of cement. The steps of few passers-by are light in search for merchandise. The music blares from discos where white drunkards climb on poles with lust, their eyes lost in an abyss, impermeable, flat. In a corner, someone asks for money. It is midday and the strollers with shorts and a camera circulate. There are no trees in the narrow street. The blaring, searing sunrays of summer give small stabbings to the skin, crashing on the windowpanes of empty shops. Not knowing what to search for, I walk up and down. Suddenly, I hear a buried murmur from the distant past, the throngs that could not sit in, that could not enter a bathroom, drink water, or eat, but one day dared to see death in the face. (In the street, there is a sense of paralysis: strollers pacing in circles. It is hard to notice their bodies in movement. They are thin like white paper, sharp and uncomfortable like sunrays.) It was their city. It still is. Now they came back to the park to dream and breathe hope. Fallen, forlorn. The streets are empty. Where is everyone? A crime is hidden under the roots of trees. A train of people could not enter the buildings. Those beaten are squatting with their eyes in shock and terror. Children are hiding their faces in their mothers' laps. The white man asks for money. He has a chair and a sign. Cars whish by in a rush, competing for the lane to be first or run the red light.

The streets are empty at night and at day unnoticed walkers roam in my neighborhood. Some come empty-handed asking for work or steal from an open garage. I can barely see any pedestrians. Porches are empty. In a deserted town the horizon expands. Where do people live? I can only hear the circular sound of metallic wheels, the whistle that takes me nowhere at the center of a floating city made up of dense abandonment. A quagmire dissolved the moment I imagine it. There is no air, no breeze, but an impenetrable gray veil like the abandoned textile mills with the workers' voices buried in a history that has never been written, only in a puppet play no one ever saw. Where are the voices? Where are the steps of those who own the land? Hidden, invisible, smothered, choked, under broken branches covered with pavement. The walkers are the color of pavement. Silence. The unpleasant insignificance of gestures.

When I hear the train I search for a rhythm, circling in that abstract, untouchable space I try to imagine again and again. The unyielding ivy wrapping itself around magnificent trunks, their branches violently cut by the electric company. They are wounded yet keep on living with humble generosity, housing tree nests. The ivy has become part of their veins, of their flowing sap. They now depend on each other like I depend on them to breathe. I could never reproduce all those shapes and colors in constant movement, in graceful sway: a symphony of crackles and squawks, of peeps and trills in myriad tones and pitches.

Why is it empty the main street of town? Where are they hidden, the spirits of the past, the throngs that swarmed and were left outside, who sat with boldness and were chased out with rage and bats, who have the tenacity of a majestic tree that survives the blows of a hatchet like the boldness and perseverance of those who survive jail and humiliation, poverty, despair? Where are those multitudes, the real owners of the land? There is a subterranean flow of pain, an invisible subway where spirits meet to talk and laugh upstairs, on the street. A cardboard theater, a coffee shop, new restaurants, white men everywhere. Where are they in the street? The trees bow down beholding in silence the ubiquitous crime. What is the sound of a crime? The cicadas chirp, the birds squawk, the leaves rustle and I stand before the windowpane looking for colors and meaning. I cling to a butterfly or the gift of a hummingbird, the blurred color of the roses, the ominous, opalescent blues of morning glories, the English ivy embracing slowly the tree and its breathing veins. Here come the axes of the electric company. There is no clemency. The terrifying crime with its syncopated noise is here again. The streets are empty. The birds have been torn from their nests by electric saws. Where are the bees? The big and the small, respectful of each other, making miracles happen in exquisite choreographies, feeding us from the dust of pollen. And the intelligence of the ivy, climbing persistently in perfectly woven expansion.

The sound of airplanes, the sound of chains, of the wheels and rails of the train in a circle far up, intangible, repeated. The sound of motion, no sound of steps, soft steps, of bodiless bodies with smiles. Where does it come from the mysterious whistle? It is clear and loud every night yet I cannot hold onto its shrill clatter. What is the sound of a prison, a block of concrete without windows?

A crow, two crows, step by step. No sound of children only of cars zooming by: metallic engines, wailing ambulances, police sirens, muffled in the distance under the cotton sky. The impenetrability of the air. Who can hear a human voice? Who is first to pass one another without conversations and time to spare? Just to contemplate the azure tones in leaves, the movement of flowers who shake their heads at midday or the dizzying phosphorescence of morning glories opening up momentarily, causing perplexity in the humid air before the society of insects.

Where do birds sleep? In tall trunks branching out into veils of emerald light. Their supple density succumbs under the balancing dance of squirrels. All kinds of insects twitter a symphony unwinding into warbles. How do I translate the greenery, the bountiful bridge that opens its arm to welcome me to tread onto leaves of grass? Its drenched, opalescent reflections grow distant, fade down toward the roots, never prickling my sight. Benumbed I then float to the cinnabars and magentas of bougainvilleas ablaze at the other South, while I sink in the wet soil and find a root in the viridian tapestries of Greensboro.

VERÓNICA GROSSI was born in Mexico City. Her poetry has appeared in publications, including *Road to Ciudad Juárez, Luvina: Literary Magazine of the Univ. of Guadalajara, International Poetry Review*, and *Anthology of Poetry 1994/1995: Mexic-Arte Museum*. She teaches Latin American literature at the University of North Carolina at Greensboro and is also a painter.

About the Cover

The cover illustration for *27 Views of Greensboro* is the work of Chapel Hill writer and artist Daniel Wallace. His illustrations have appeared in many publications, including the *Los Angeles Times, Italian Vanity Fair,* and *Our State* magazine. He is the author and illustrator of *The Cat's Pajamas,* a children's book published by Inkshares. He illustrated the book covers of *27 Views of Hillsborough, 27 Views of Chapel Hill, 27 Views of Asheville, 27 Views of Durham, 27 Views of Raleigh,* and *27 Views of Charlotte,* all published by Eno Publishers. He also illustrated *Papadaddy's Book for New Fathers,* by Clyde Edgerton.

Award-winning Books from Eno Publishers

27 Views of Charlotte
The Queen City in Prose & Poetry
INTRODUCTION BY JACK CLAIBORNE
$14.95/226 pages

27 Views of Raleigh
The City of Oaks in Prose & Poetry
INTRODUCTION BY WILTON BARNHARDT
$15.95/224 pages

27 Views of Durham
The Bull City in Prose & Poetry
INTRODUCTION BY STEVE SCHEWEL
$15.95/216 pages

27 Views of Asheville
A Southern Mountain Town in Prose & Poetry
INTRODUCTION BY ROB NEUFELD
$15.95/216 pages

27 Views of Chapel Hill
A Southern University Town in Prose & Poetry
INTRODUCTION BY DANIEL WALLACE
$16.50/240 pages

27 Views of Hillsborough
A Southern Town in Prose & Poetry
INTRODUCTION BY MICHAEL MALONE
$15.95/216 pages
Gold IPPY Book Award, Best Anthology
Gold Eric Hoffer Book Award, Culture

Chapel Hill in Plain Sight
Notes from the Other Side of the Tracks
DAPHNE ATHAS
$16.95/246 pages

Undaunted Heart
The True Story of a Southern Belle & a Yankee General
SUZY BARILE
$16.95/238 pages
Silver IPPY Book Award, Best Regional Nonfiction

Brook Trout & the Writing Life
The Intermingling of Fishing & Writing in a Novelist's Life
CRAIG NOVA
$15.95/152 pages

Rain Gardening in the South
Ecologically Designed Gardens for Drought,
Deluge & Everything in Between
HELEN KRAUS & ANNE SPAFFORD
$19.95/144 pages
Gold Book Award, Garden Writers Association
Silver Book Award, Garden Writers Association
Silver Benjamin Franklin Book Award
Honorable Mention, Eric Hoffer Book Award

CPSIA information can be obtained
at www.ICGtesting.com
Printed in the USA
JSHW020231210723
45111JS00004B/15

9 780989 609210